DISC ||||||||||||||||||||||||||||
D0685028

"Kelley Nikondeha is my favorite kind of theologian—a
hybrid of poet and prophet, both mystical and yet very much
planted in our world. This book is a radical look at belonging, and it will change all of us who are looking for ways to
expand our tables."

> — **D. L. MAYFIELD**
> author of *Assimilate or Go Home:
> Notes from a Failed Missionary on
> Rediscovering Faith*

"Nikondeha effortlessly interweaves her lived experiences
of adoption with provocative biblical stories and a daring
theological imagination. So good!"

> — **DREW G. I. HART**
> author of *Trouble I've Seen:
> Changing the Way the Church
> Views Racism*

"As an orphan, daughter, and adoptive mother, Kelley brings
a depth of experience and clarity of pen to this work of lived
theology. If you're looking to adopt a holistic theology of orphan care, grab this book."

> — **SETH HAINES**
> author of *Coming Clean:
> A Story of Faith*

"Through the metaphor of adoption, Kelley Nikondeha calls us to a vision of family that is generous, inclusive, and always ready to add another chair. This is the vision of the family of God I long for."

— **IDELETTE MCVICKER**
founder and editor-in-chief of
SheLovesmagazine.com

"I am so thankful for this work from the brilliant mind of Kelley Nikondeha. Theologically rich yet entirely accessible, her *Adopted* will surely become a favorite among church leaders and laypeople alike. It's easily one of my favorite books of the year."

— **NISH WEISETH**
author of *Speak: How Your Story Can Change the World*

ADOPTED

The Sacrament of Belonging
in a Fractured World

KELLEY NIKONDEHA

WILLIAM B. EERDMANS PUBLISHING COMPANY
GRAND RAPIDS, MICHIGAN

Wm. B. Eerdmans Publishing Co.
2140 Oak Industrial Drive NE, Grand Rapids, Michigan 49505
www.eerdmans.com

26 25 24 23 22 21 20 19 18 17   1 2 3 4 5 6 7 8 9 10

ISBN 978-0-8028-7425-2

Library of Congress Cataloging-in-Publication Data

Names: Nikondeha, Kelley, 1969– author.
Title: Adopted : the sacrament of belonging in a fractured world /
    Kelley Nikondeha.
Description: Grand Rapids : Eerdmans Publishing Co., 2017. |
    Includes bibliographical references.
Identifiers: LCCN 2017008848 | ISBN 9780802874252 (pbk. : alk. paper)
Subjects: LCSH: Adoption (Theology) | Belonging (Social psychology)
Classification: LCC BT165 .N48 2017 | DDC 204/.41—dc23
    LC record available at https://lccn.loc.gov/2017008848

For the company of the adopted,
the relinquished and the redeemed.

This is our sacrament.
We sip from the chalice daily.
We imbibe God's grace with each taste.

May our sacrament and our struggle
be a gift to a world hungry for belonging.

Contents

Foreword

Mother Teresa once said that the circle we draw around family is too small. We put limits on love. Because our vision isn't as big as God's, we can end up spiritually short-sighted.

We reduce family to biology or nationality or ethnicity. We put up picket fences and build walls along our borders. We use the language of "us" and "them," and we draw lines in the sand.

Kelley Nikondeha is the perfect person to set us free from our myopia and tunnel vision. She helps open our eyes to the boundless love of God. This book is about belonging. It is about the limitless hospitality of God, which has the power to transform us into people who extend the same hospitality to others.

Kelley was adopted at birth, something that has deepened her sense of what it is to be chosen. That also means her love is big, and the circle she draws around family is wide. She's the adoptive mother of two kids from Burundi, a constant reminder that God specializes in the "supranatural" as much as the natural.

As I read this book, I was reminded of the words of author and priest Henri Nouwen in *With Open Hands*:

> Across all barriers of land and language, wealth and poverty, knowledge and ignorance, we are one, created from the same dust, subject to the same laws, and destined for the same end. With this compassion you can say, "In the face of the oppressed I recognize my own face, and in the hands of the oppressors I recognize my own hands. Their flesh is my flesh, their blood is my blood, their pain is my pain, their smile is my smile."

Throughout these pages, Kelley fleshes out what it means to belong to each other and to the God who made us. She takes readers on a tour through Scripture, beginning with a baby in danger—Moses—whose desperate mother floated him down a river only to find him rescued and adopted by Pharaoh's daughter. And that's just the beginning. All through Scripture, Kelley traces the thread of adoption and belonging.

It's a beautiful book—for people who are thinking of building a family together, and for people who are looking for family. It shows that the relentless love of God cannot be contained. It doesn't stop at borders, or walls, or picket fences.

At the heart of the Christian faith is the idea that we are to be "born again," as Jesus said to Nicodemus in the Gospel of John. To be born again means we have a new definition of family. As Jesus says, "What is born of the flesh is flesh, and what is born of the Spirit is spirit." No longer is family limited to DNA.

And it was Jesus who, when told his mother and brothers were outside, spoke these words: "Who is my mother, and who are my brothers?" (Matt. 12:48-50). Whoever does the will of God—they are family to him, and to us. He's not disrespecting his family—he's just challenging the narrow vision that might be constricting our definitions of who belongs. Our circles around family might just be too small.

One of the things that Mother Teresa taught the world, and embodied so brilliantly, is the broad definition of family. When I worked with her and the sisters in Calcutta, I saw it firsthand. She rescued orphans abandoned in train stations and took in teenage moms. I even met grown men who had been raised by her. One of them explained to me that this is how she got her name. He went on to tell me stories from his childhood and show me things she had given him, just like a kid talking about his mom. She was "Mom" before she was "Mother Teresa." She made the circle around family much bigger.

Kelley writes about that same wide circle. Her words expand our vision and deepen our sense of how loved by God we truly are. And she dares us to demonstrate that same generous love to the world we live in, a world desperately in need of love—ripped apart by war, hatred, famine, and disease, its people suffering under the residue of slavery and racism, its families torn asunder by poverty and injustice.

And in the face of all this, there is hope. That hope springs from the sacrament of adoption, which Kelley calls "a sacrament of resistance." The belonging that she describes allows us to rest in the confidence that we are beloved. It pushes back against all that divides the world. In Kelley's words, "Adoption is one way we dare to stitch the world back together."

This book has the power to enlarge the circle around our families—or, better yet, to erase the circle altogether, so that our vision of family is as wide and as expansive as God's.

Shane Claiborne

Introduction

In an unphotographed moment, I entered the church. Soon after my birth, the good women of Holy Family Adoption Agency in Los Angeles made sure I was baptized. A priest sprinkled holy water on my forehead, and the church embraced me. I slipped into God's family almost unnoticed. This was my first adoption.

A few weeks later, a woman scooped me out of the white-wicker bassinet in the viewing room of the adoption agency and claimed me as her own. Her physical emptiness prepared the way for my fullness; now I was twice adopted. By the time we left the building, with her cradling me in the crook of her arm, I belonged. That's how sacraments tend to work—altering reality in an instant.

When Neil Armstrong stepped onto the moon in the summer of 1969, I was at home, bouncing on the knee of my paternal grandmother. The Americans were winning the race to space, one front of the Cold War. But the world unraveled on other fronts with proxy wars, the arms race, and an emerging binary way of seeing anyone not like us as bad, wrong—or worse. We were losing our capacity for connection, for belonging. I grew up in a world of us versus them, where the lines of demarcation were clear and increasingly impenetrable.

As I grew, I discovered my story to be a counter-narrative. Relinquished by one. Received by another. Early on, I was already learning an alternative story about family formation that would set the trajectory of my life. I belonged despite biological difference. My family pushed past the fractured ways of the world with a fierce fidelity. In doing so, they taught me that anyone could belong, could be family—and I believed them. What growing up adopted taught me is that I could find belonging in unexpected places. It is with that adoptive awareness that I learned both a life lesson and a scriptural truth: belonging is a choice, a series of habits, and a way of life that cultivates healing.

Jesus is the only-begotten Son of the Father. These are the words of the Apostles' Creed, the words we speak and the way we affirm how Jesus uniquely generates from God in a direct, almost biological, way. No one else is God-begotten. All of us, the Apostle Paul tells us, are adopted into God's family. We are God's children by another means. Because that is the essence of our relationship to God—our adoption—exploring what that means is vital to better understanding our membership in God's family and its implications for our connection to one another.

Clear insights into adoption also allow us to explore the anatomy of belonging and learn practices that cultivate connection and create community in unlikely places. Those with tenure in the company of the adopted are practitioners of belonging. They have much to teach us about how to extend our family to embrace others, be it in the church or in our neighborhood.

I've lived as an adopted person for over forty years, and my husband and I adopted our two children from Burundi over eleven years ago. So I've experienced firsthand the deeply formative work of adoption. I've also studied Scripture for decades, watching how the metaphor of adoption operates in God's story of deliverance. I am convinced that adoption is a potent metaphor for us as we seek to build community and repair the divisions in our world. Adoption isn't only about orphans; it is about family, God's family.

When he was in first grade, I found my son lying in the fetal position on my bedroom floor one morning. I dropped down beside him and saw his tears. "Mom, my birth mother needs me. I love you, but I have to go to her."

"Son, that's not how adoption works," I said. As I rubbed his tiny back, I reminded him that we didn't know where his birth mother lived or exactly why she had let him go. Poised to launch into my speech about being grateful for his adopted family, I was soon shushed by the Spirit. *Let him have his own experience of adoption.*

Taking a deep breath, I swallowed my speech. I brought him close and let him cry. "Why do you think she needs you now?" I asked.

"She's hungry, Mama. I need to bring her food," he said as his compassion surged. Before I could insert any comment, he added, "I can share my own food with her—I can eat less so she can have enough." Listening to my son, I learned that there isn't just one adoption, but rather many adoptions, each one unique.

Adoption is complicated. As familiar with heartache as with hospitality and over time stripped of all heroics, it can reveal humble truths. Belonging isn't easy or guaranteed; there are a hundred ways it can go wrong. But there are as many ways it can go right, as strangers are transformed into relatives. Family formation is always a risk, but a worthy one. That's why we wrestle and contend for the blessings, as Jacob did in Genesis: to know the sacrament of belonging.

This is how adoption works—like a sacrament, that visible sign of an inner grace. It's a thin place where we see that we are different and yet not entirely foreign to one another.

We are relatives not by blood, but by mystery. All that divides us as nations, ethnicities, and religious traditions is like a vapor quickly extinguished in light of our adoption into God's family.

The lines between *us* and *them* are quite entrenched. We see others as different and cannot imagine holding anything in common with them. How could there ever be a connection with people so unlike us? Adoption cuts right through those binary ways of thinking. A child, no matter what family or country she comes from, is now your daughter. You find yourself caring for her and each day realizing a bit more how alike you are in your needs, desires, and delights. What if connecting with others is like adoption, a matter of choosing to make room for them in your life? What if the lessons of adoption are the lessons of belonging and have wider implications for how we can, in fact, push past binaries and become family?

The everyday experience of adopted living teaches us about belonging beyond boundaries. The metaphor embraced by the Scriptures has the capacity to reshape our practice of family. It introduces us to the more extensive family God envisions. And it shows us that adoption is a visible sign to the world that God continues to transform widows into mothers, orphans into daughters and sons, making all of us kin.

Adoption has shaped me as a daughter, a mother, and a neighbor. Both lived experience and biblical reflection have taught me that adoption transforms us. Despite its complications, adoption has great gifts to offer the orphaned among us. And as God's adopted ones, we are all learning how to embody a truer kind of family and make our way home to the Father's house together. Jesus promises there is room enough for all of us at the family table.

CHAPTER ONE

Roots

B ack in the Garden of Eden, the epicenter of the cosmos, God reached into the earth to form Adam. All of the biological matter residing in the dark loam, the seeds and soil and nutrients, became part of humanity. Our first biological link is to soil, or so the story goes.

What this original story cracks open for us is the reminder that we are deeply related to creation. We are a swirl of soil and seeds, skin and bone, divinity and mystery. It is good to remember that we belonged to a place before we belonged to a people.

Out of the Garden and into the wider landscape of Scripture, we begin to see those stories of our origins unfold. Beyond clan and tribe, something curious takes hold. Complexity forms at the fringes of bloodlines, and we witness something elusive yet generative at work. Family bonds are created within tribes but also completely apart from them. The tendrils of filial connection are reaching out beyond national borders and twining around different ethnicities to shape a more expansive family.

When it comes to describing *belonging* in Scripture, *family* is the metaphor of choice. Adam and Eve are the original family generating from the heart of the Trinity. The Holy Family enters the scene in the Gospel accounts. Between them are generations of families with tangled stories of fidelity and estrangement, barrenness and birth, sibling rivalries and reconciliations. It is through this metaphor that we witness belonging.

When I was a child, every Sunday morning found me sitting with other kids in a semi-circle on the carpet in the fellowship hall of St. Nicholas Catholic Church. We listened, eyes wide, as our Sunday school teacher told stories out of the big illustrated Bible. Like an oscillating fan, she'd move back and forth to ensure we could see all the heroes and heroines in water-colored action. We craned to catch a glimpse of Miriam dancing across the Red Sea, Joseph strutting in his technicolor coat, David with his slingshot, Queen Esther on her throne.

Though we were thousands of years apart, I still knew I was born into the world like them, even Esther, who was "born for such a time as this." I also knew that my mother wasn't the one who delivered me so much as the one who received me. Perhaps this explains my attraction to the life of Moses, both a liberator and an adopted child—he embodied a belonging that was familiar to me. My mother didn't pull me out of a river, but I imagined the current that brought me to her was just as mystical and intentional. Like the other children clustered around the great big book every Sunday, I looked to see where I fit into God's story.

My own story positioned me to notice adoption at work in Scripture. I saw it not as an invisible metaphor to be unearthed, but as a dynamic to be recognized. In Scripture, adoption meddles with genealogies, subverts oppressive empires, secures imperial inheritances, and opens new possibilities for who can be family. Fracture opens the narrative, and adoption isn't far behind as a means of repair and integration. As an adult I remain convinced that in order to understand the biblical exploration of belonging, we must include the metaphor of adoption. When I listened to each biblical family story told by my Sunday school teacher, what I intuitively suspected was confirmed—blood isn't thicker than water. When you factor in adoption, bloodlines don't have the final say in who belongs in your family. Belonging, not blood, is definitive.

Idelette sat on the red couch in her Vancouver living room, sipping rooibos tea from her homeland. In the bright morning sunlight, we spoke of adoption's healing potential in the world. It wasn't an uncommon conversation for us. We had met in Kenya at the Amahoro Gathering, a conversation my husband Claude and I host for African thinkers and practitioners. And ever since, she and I had been talking about Jesus, justice, and our long walk to freedom.

"I want to offer better language for those in the company of the adopted," I told her over my cup of red tea. "I want to expand our conversation about adoption so that we understand its formative work in us and, by extension, in the world."

"I want to be a part of that conversation," she chimed in as she walked toward the kitchen. "After all, I'm adopted, too!"

For the record, Idelette is not adopted in the primary sense of the word. She knows it; I know it. But she insisted, "Paul says that God adopts us—that would make me adopted, and so your conversation would matter to me." She pulled the blueberry muffins out of the oven, plated them, and offered them to me. But by now I was feeling defensive, unable to return her easy smile or enjoy the muffins.

Yes, Paul did employ the language of adoption in his letters, but to a different effect, I assured her. "It's *as if* you are adopted by God. It's a simile, really," I insisted.

She broke open a muffin in her hands. "I'm pretty sure I'm adopted by God," she said, taking a bite and catching a crumb with her finger.

In that moment she became a trespasser, and I was determined to defend my birthright. I didn't have a biological leg to stand on, but I was a full-fledged member of the company of the adopted. She could learn from my adoptive experience but not claim it as her own. Her insistence was an invasion.

It would be many months later, when the two of us were sitting in my living room, before I could tell her, over a plate of hummus and carrots, that she was right. I had spent the better part of my summer in Burundi following the adoption metaphor throughout Scripture and studying Paul's letters to discover what she intuitively knew. Paul didn't soften adoption into a simile; he used the full force of metaphor. We are *all* adopted by God. Theologically, Idelette and I are both adopted children.

In a temporal sense, I am adopted and she is not. I was relinquished by my first mother and never knew my father, and I don't know my family's medical history. I've learned how to be a daughter without reflecting my adoptive parents' likeness in the mirror. This is part of the adoptive experience I alone know, one that Idelette can't completely embody. And that's why I felt the heat of offense when she first mentioned a shared sacrament.

But ontologically we *do* share this sacrament of belonging. Paul says that the spirit of adoption has been given to each of us, making us daughters of God and sisters to one another. And I know something in me had to change in order to acknowledge that truth. Maybe it was hard for me to imagine adoption without relinquishment, to allow Idelette to step into the redemptive arc of belonging without the loss. But I cannot bar God from generosity. The Father gives good gifts, even adoptive ones, to others. My own understanding of the company of the adopted was too narrow. I couldn't hoard the sacrament of belonging any more than the Hebrews could hoard daily-given manna. If I tried to keep the adoptive goodness to myself, I'd betray the generosity of our Father.

A friend once said to me that when you read the Apostle Paul's letter to the Romans at a certain slant, it almost looks like God adopted Abraham.[1] This elder of Ur, plucked out of genealogical obscurity to be God's own, becomes an "ancestor of all who believe" by another divine orchestration. Abraham becomes "as if" he were God's firstborn, with the privilege, the blessing, and the vast promise of an inheritance. It's grown on me, this idea of Abraham being "as if adopted" by God, providing my imagination with another window to view God's limitless capacity to forge belonging beyond our natural boundaries.

In his letter to the Roman church, Paul described how God's family underwent a deep transformation. There was a time when Israel—and only Israel—could be described as the children of God. They alone bore the mark of circumcision, a sign of their covenant with God, setting them apart as God's unique people on the earth. They possessed the Law, the history, and the genealogy back to Abraham. Israel's lineage was uncontested.

The advent of Jesus changed all this. No longer did Israel have pride of place among the tribes of the earth, doling out the blessings for lesser nations. Now the uncircumcised were circumcised not by the knife, but by keeping God's covenant. There was no longer a distinction between Jews and Greeks, said the apostle.

In showing us this family makeover, Paul points to Father Abraham's story. He recounts how Abraham acted in faith *before* he was circumcised and God reckoned him as righteous—just like that—in his uncircumcised condition. Only *after* the reckoning was Abraham circumcised. Why? So that Abraham would become our common ancestor, the father to all who believe. He has uncircumcision in common with some, circumcision in common with others, but what holds this expanded family together is faith. According to Paul, we belong to each other, a family shaped by faith, not physical marks.

Reading in Paul's letter, we learn that all of Abraham's descendants in faith will share in God's promised inheritance. For that initial Roman gathering of believers, nothing would have been more coveted than a real inheritance. And now both Jews and Greeks will share in Abraham's promise and inherit the world—as long as they believe in this God. Biology, it seems, has shifted in importance for the family of faith.

Lean across the generations and hear Abraham's echo in Isaiah—eunuchs and foreigners find a place in the New Jerusalem if they keep God's covenant and keep the Sabbath. God's family continues to grow, moving beyond tribe and clan. Lean in further still, and your ear might catch the words of the God who prefers Jacob to Esau, Abel's sacrifice over Cain's, the One willing to subvert birth orders, dismantle hierarchies, and dethrone patriarchy. This is the very One who reimagines genealogies, weaving in the abused and outcast Tamar, Rahab the Canaanite prostitute, and Ruth the Moabite to form a family that reflects the Father's own diverse and generous image.

From the faith of Abraham to the unorthodox genealogies, the Apostle Paul reveals the truth hinted at throughout the generations—we belong by believing, not by biology. All who believe, all who keep covenant, all who want in can be grafted into this family tree. As our eyes open, we begin to see a more expansive kind of family. By comparison, our notion of family, defined by bloodlines and ethnicities, begins to look narrow and far too exclusive to resemble God's largess.

Abraham's story is only the beginning of the adoption narratives we unearth in the biblical root system. Arcane adoption formulas are embedded in the Hebrew Bible. In Genesis we overhear Rachel planning the adoption of the child of her maid, Bilhah, as she commands Jacob to ". . . go in to her, that she may *bear upon my knees* and I too may have children through her."[2] We witness the patriarch Joseph adopting his grandchildren, born in Egypt, so that they will be full heirs of Israel,[3] with the same formula: ". . . *born on Joseph's knees.*" The image is that of a father putting the children on his knees, admiring and acknowledging these as his kin. Much later, in the book of Ruth, it is Naomi, a full-blooded Israelite, who brings her grandson ". . . *and [lays] him on her bosom*" to ensure he will not be left out of the lineage due to the foreign status of his mother, Ruth, a Moabite.[4]

When I read through these histories, it seems to me that Israel had a tradition of adoption. Whether to address a foreign birth or a foreign mother, adoption ensured children belonged to the tribe and would not be disinherited. Adoption was a remedy of sorts. According to the stories of Scripture, it both meddled in and mended families.

If God writes straight using crooked lines, as Desmond Tutu says, has God's intended family been taking shape by unexpected means all along?

On Epiphany Sunday a few years ago, I took one last look at the manger scene perched on the altar of the local cathedral in my neighborhood. Joseph knelt over his newborn son. Like any other father, he looked astonished at the strength of his wife, mesmerized by the arrival of this child. In this adoption scene, a father on his knees received a son as his own. This was how Joseph first experienced fatherhood. And it was through the story of Joseph that I first recognized Jesus as *the Adopted One.*

God rooted his own Son into the biblical story as the son of David and a son of Abraham through Jesse's son, Joseph. His divine paternity would be known only to a few—for the moment. In the Gospels we learn of the divine intervention and the human agency involved in the birth of Jesus. God created belonging through both biological and adoptive means.

Early on in her pregnancy, Mary knew this child was somehow set apart. The angel Gabriel made that clear (that is, as clear as possible, given the shift required of Mary to understand that her womb carried a child conceived by the Holy Spirit). Joseph soon learned this child was not his or any other man's; an angelic dream confirmed a holy meddling. "She will bear a son," the messenger said, "and *you* are to name him Jesus. . . ." It would be Joseph, and not God in a voice from on high, who would first announce the name of this boy to the family. Culturally and theologically, it matters who makes that announcement. When Joseph named Mary's son, the boy became his own in the eyes of the community—maybe even in the eyes of God. To name him was to claim him as his firstborn child, thus locating Jesus in Joseph's lineage.

So it is that Jesus possesses Mary's biology and Joseph's genealogy, all the while carrying God's progeny into the world—in the fullest expression of family.

One story appearing in three of the Four Gospels makes more sense to us when we see Jesus as the Adopted One at work. As the Gospel of Mark records it, Jesus is in his hometown, healing and teaching. His mother and brothers arrive at the scene and begin calling out to him, trying to get his attention above the noise of the crowd. Soon the people chime in: "Jesus, your mother and brothers are outside asking for you." Jesus stops. He looks around at the packed audience, then asks, "Who is my mother? Who are my brothers?" To those surrounding him, it seems obvious—they are the ones outside calling for you.

"Whoever does the will of God is my brother, my sister, even my mother," Jesus says, bringing the crowd into confused silence. What an audacious thing to say on this

Palestinian street in the first century—to suggest that any other affiliation could rival that of family! In the mind-set of the crowd, nothing trumps family, nothing supersedes commitment to your blood and bone, your tribe and clan.

But Jesus isn't diminishing his mother or brothers in public. He's simply describing his own experience of family. This is what Joseph taught him: Anyone can be your family if you choose to live with fidelity toward one another. Jesus was going public with how those in the company of the adopted function. In doing so, he expanded the crowd's understanding of who could be family, for those who had ears to hear or eyes to see what he saw when he looked at the crowd.

Did Mary and her sons experience those words of Jesus as insult? Maybe they were exasperated by his antics or tired of waiting for him—but I suspect his description of family didn't offend them. After all, they all lived under Joseph's roof. This was a family knit together by adoption. Jesus was as much a son to Mary as he was a sibling to his brothers and sisters. This family was a testament to another way of belonging.

I've never found this story shocking, though I can see why it might be to others. But my own particular circumstances help me understand an aspect of Jesus' embrace, as he threw his arms open wide to stretch the definition of family to include everyone. Maybe it's my shared adoptive history with Jesus that allows me to so readily accept his idea of family largess.

I grew up as an only child, but I had a bevy of cousins, courtesy of my mother's three sisters. Uncle Pat and Auntie Kathy's kids were the closest in both age and geographic proximity, so we spent most of our childhood together. We crammed into the backseat of the van when we carpooled to Old Mission Catholic School; we shared holiday celebrations and picnics at the beach. I loved propping the littlest one on my hip and listening to the silly jokes of the only boy among us. It never occurred to me that they were pseudo-family. They were my cousins in every way that mattered.

I watch my own children reincarnate this relationship with their Burundian cousins. Every summer they meet a new cluster of cousins, thanks to the generous size of my husband's family. Last year we hosted another branch of the family tree at a garden party in our Bujumbura home. The kids ran round and round, played basketball in our makeshift half-court, and drank too many Fantas. Emma meandered over to my side late in the day. "Are these my real cousins, Mom? The blood kind?"

"No, not the blood kind. Does that matter?" I asked.

Her smile came first, then her answer: "No! They're my cousins because we say so!" And she joined them for the dance party as the music started playing.

Sometimes you learn early that they're your cousins because Mama says so—and you believe her. It's a lesson I first learned from Joseph.

As I spend time reading about the life of Jesus, I notice that adoption, as a modality, unlocks something that birth alone does not. In theological terms, blood is not thicker than water. The experience of living as an adopted person within a family makes this utterly clear. Every time the family gathers at the breakfast table, the counter-narrative of non-biological belonging is incarnated. We are connected by more than genes; we are relatives by daily fidelity and even deeper mysteries.

My own sense of belonging, bookended by my adoptive parents and my own adopted children, testifies to this connection. I carry my mother's values; my children incarnate the Nikondeha character, whether on the playground or round the dinner table. Years of shared memories fuse our family together. We bear an indelible mark of filial bonding not limited by physicality. For adopted ones, the reality, not just the possibility, of connection between those who share no biological link is undeniable.

Jesus experienced that adopted reality and learned, in the most human way, that anyone could be his mother, brother, sister—or father.[5] And we see evidence of that. Joseph was as necessary in the life and development of Jesus as Mary. Joseph not only gave Jesus a name and a genealogy; he gave Jesus a lived experience of adoption that allowed him to confidently proclaim a new way of belonging. The Holy Family enacted this adoptive dynamic and embodied the truth of the ever-expansive family of God.

Adoption is what opened the door, what allowed Jesus to develop a new awareness regarding bloodlines, ethnicity, and shared geography as he walked the streets of Nazareth. Maybe these things weren't as determinative after all. What if family connection happened with and even without those elements? Jesus, the Adopted One, began to crack open and reshape the definition of family.

God the Father gave his Son many divine gifts, but only Joseph adopted him. It may be that Jesus' adopted heritage, empowered by the Spirit, allowed him to enact the kind of inclusive welcome of God's Kingdom that the prophets who came before him only dreamed of.

Standing amid the crowd that day, Jesus sounded a bit like Isaiah. Listeners may well have made that comparison. Despite Isaiah's vision for a radical inclusion, the Jews hadn't yet fashioned a city devoid of ethnic divisions, partisan fractures, and xenophobia. Yet there stood the Adopted One, helping us cross over to a new understanding of family, community, and Kingdom.

Whoever keeps covenant. Whoever does the will of my Father. Whoever believes. Isaiah, Jesus, and Paul all sing variations of the same song. What the prophets hinted at, Jesus says straight out. And Paul recognizes it, seeing how God is weaving this family of belonging from the time of Abraham. Anyone can become a member of God's family—this is the base line for their song.

Jesus embodied this kind of family largess. Watch him, and you'll notice the company he kept. He was at ease with street kids, sick people, prostitutes—the outcasts of society. He welcomed women, foreigners, and Roman functionaries. He dined with the religious elite and partisan politicians. This is what you'd expect from someone unlimited by the boundary markers of ethnicity, class, and clan. Anyone could be close as kin to Jesus.

Augustus, emperor of the Roman Empire, was the adopted son of Julius Caesar. He was a distinguished soldier, engaged in the final military campaigns that created the empire. Caesar adopted him to ensure that the newly formed empire would remain in the family. When it came to securing succession, Caesar took no chances, using adoption as the mechanism to guarantee the imperial inheritance.[6]

This wasn't a fluke of history. Augustus also employed adoption to secure succession when he adopted Gaius and Lucius. Then Tiberius adopted Germanicus and Nero to continue the dynasty. Imperial families wielded adoption as a tool of the empire to ensure their throne always had an unquestioned heir.

Jesus was born under Augustus and crucified under Tiberius. And the Apostle Paul lived through the reign of these men. The places where his letters circulated—those communities in the region of Galatia, in Rome, and in the surrounding areas—all endured this dynasty. The genealogies and family stories of the emperors would have been well known and often repeated in the streets. It's fair to say that everyone knew which ones were adopted and why.

Adoption was clearly not a foreign concept in the Greco-Roman world. But it's important to note how differently Paul and his communities would have heard that word! Our contemporary concept of adopting an infant, with the connotations of nurture, care, and compassion, is, in fact, anachronistic. The common understanding of adoption in the Greco-Roman world would have been functional: it was a tool of the elite (especially the emperors) to secure succession, legacy, and inheritance. Adopted sons were pulled into a bigger story and expected to fulfill an imperial purpose. In those times, adoption was about the coalescing and movement of power, not the rescue of orphans.

Paul uses the metaphor of adoption in Galatians and Romans, coupling that with the metaphor of inheritance in each instance. And against the Greco-Roman background of the imperial families, this makes perfect sense. When

we take a macro-view of these adoption texts, we acknowledge Paul's declaration that God adopts us to secure God's
own kingdom of love across the world. *We are God's adopted
ones.* We are functionaries of God's Kingdom and full heirs
of God's promise. But we realize we are more than that when
we witness Paul stretch the adoption metaphor beyond
power and politics to point to family connection. We are not
mere imperial functionaries; we are also family members.
As family, we recognize one another as siblings and are invited into filial solidarity as *adopted ones.*

Recently I mused aloud to my husband about how proud his
parents must be of him and his work in Burundi, his homeland. I began to list the first few things that came to mind:
his working to provide food security, homes, health services,
and education for many rural families; his helping build a
health clinic and a trade school in a nearby province; and
his securing identity cards for thousands of Batwa women
and men.

"Aren't they proud?" I pressed.

He gave me a thin smile. "They know I'm doing good
work, but they would be more proud if I was doing it for
our family in our ancestral home." Claude explained that
helping Batwa communities instead of the Nikondeha family clan in a nearby province confuses his parents. Yes, it's

better than becoming a thief or an addict. But it would make their joy complete if he would concentrate his efforts within the tribe, assisting Tutsi villages and their relatives.

Claude's parents are two of the most generous and loving people I know. But it's no surprise that they hold to the tribalism that has divided the country in years of violent civil war. Sometimes the good news of creating viable communities stops at the clan's edge.

Here is what Claude knows deeper than words: All Burundians are his relatives. He stands in solidarity with these families, be they Batwa, Hutu, or Tutsi. He pours out his life for them because they are irrevocably his own. Once he told me that his very humanity depended on how he loved these families. As an adopted one of God, he knows, like Jesus, like Paul, there is no basis for division along clan or ethnic lines.

In the wake of the deaths of Michael Brown, Eric Garner, and too many others, the Black Lives Matter movement emerged across the nation. Young activists took to the streets and social media to decry the injustices their communities suffered, especially the onslaught of police brutality raining down on their families. Echoes of the civil rights movement could be heard as voices rose in protest from Baltimore, Ferguson, Chicago, and other cities across the country.

One voice speaking into the racial reckoning is social

psychologist Christena Cleveland. She was invited to join other African-American activists and clergy at Urbana 2015, a mission conversation co-hosted by three Christian associations, to speak about race and the church. Even in the church, she said, we gravitate to homogeneous groups. White Christians tend to stay together, and black believers do the same. Breaking out of our in-group is hard, sociologically speaking.[7] We are more kind to those in our group and are more likely to offer them the benefit of the doubt in confusing situations. But when it comes to those who aren't part of *us,* we believe that their motives are different, and we assume the worst of them. From Cleveland's observations it was easy to make connections to our current situation riddled with racial tension and the increasing hurdles (and history) between us.

Offering instruction from the life of Jesus, Cleveland opened the Gospel of Matthew to 12:46–50, the same text we considered earlier in this chapter. She challenged the students in that auditorium, amid a fresh iteration of the civil rights movement, to consider what family Jesus was inviting them into. "Who is part of your *us?*" she asked. Including *them* in our *us,* we would begin to treat them differently because they would be like family.

According to Cleveland's reading of the text, Jesus redefines *us* and pushes against society's definitions of who is valued, prioritized, and privileged. Before leaving the auditorium, she posed this final question: "Who is part of your family, and how will the world know?" This question haunts me still.

Family, adoption, and inheritance: in exploring belonging, Scripture braids together these three root metaphors. We see hints of these metaphors in Abraham, our common ancestor. We witness Jesus, the Adopted One, stretching the definition of family. And we see the Apostle Paul instructing the early church, telling them they are adopted ones now related not only to God, but also to one another. He tells them that they are the new humanity, the inclusive family of God.

The stories of Scripture lead us to understand our belonging to God's family through adoption, full heirs to our Father's world. As heirs, we participate in extending God's Kingdom of peace. As family, we recognize others as siblings who ought to be treated as such. As adopted ones, we extend that magnanimous belonging to others.

True belonging has never been limited to physical means or markers. Through each new generation, God has shown us that family membership is inclusive, generous, and diverse. Each new story stretches our imagination and challenges our capacity to embrace others as family. Adoption points to an ever-extending family that crosses boundaries of all sorts, excluding no one.

Claude, Idelette, and my own parents have shown me

that anyone can be your family. It is the daily lesson I hope I am teaching my own children. Adoption imbues belonging with elasticity—we know there is always room for more at the table and more in the family. As we shape our own communities of belonging, we have to run to keep up with the divine largess, since God keeps growing his family with great creativity and an ever-greater reach.

CHAPTER TWO

Relinquish

Adoption begins in the dark. It begins with the decision to let go of a small one you're only beginning to love, but cannot keep. For so many women it's a kind of darkness, after months of gestating these fragile lives within our own bodies, to realize love might look like letting go.

We don't expect love to look like relinquishment. Often we say that when mothers let go, they abandon their babies, reject their children. Some paint these women as heartless monsters who walked away when things got tough. But few birth mothers would describe their act of relinquishment in such terms.

These women open the door to piercing questions about the nature of relinquishment not only in adoption, but also in the larger landscape of belonging. Might relinquishment be part of the architecture of belonging and not just an unfortunate anomaly? Does letting go prepare us for coming close? Could relinquishment be a seedbed of sorts, a rich soil for redemption?

Relinquishment arrives uninvited, often in the wake of injustice. Biblical narrative offers an early record of the Hebrew women living across the Nile River from Pharaoh's house. They knew this truth all too well because of his harsh edict: every son born to a Hebrew woman was to be thrown into that river. How many let go of sons by force? Who were those unnamed women wailing under the swollen moon? One name, one story is given to help us understand the contours of letting go.

During this time, a Hebrew woman named Jochebed had given birth to a son. For months she had carried him in her belly, knowing the edict, and she birthed him with the stealthy assistance of the midwives. As long as she could, she hid him in her home. She studied his yet-unnamed face in the moonlight, singing old lullabies into his fresh spirit as she nursed him with her milk.

But the day dawned when he was too big to hide, his lungs too robust to hush. And keeping him wasn't an option. So Jochebed needed to decide soon how to nip his budding life—or risk the soldiers drowning him.

Such is the hardship of living under the unjust mechanisms of the empire, often fueled by the fears of one Pharaoh or another. One woman finds herself forced into a corner, her babe buried in her chest, wondering what love looks like under such pressing, oppressive circumstances.

So Jochebed made a decision. At first light she took her son to the edge of the Nile River. While the world still slumbered, she'd sing a final song to him before doing the unthinkable thing that injustice required of her.

Her sweet-scented son curled into the crook of her arm as she scrambled down the embankment. Standing in the muddy space between dirt and water, she allowed herself one last look at him, seeing the goodness of creation on his cheeks in the sun's first glance. In that moment she knew what love looked like—it was God recognizing the goodness of her son, too. And love would conspire to save this boy from the grave of The Great River.

After constructing a basket of reeds, Jochebed placed her son on a bed of tender papyrus leaves. Then she bent low, the water lapping at her knees, and launched her son into the Nile. She sent him away from her, away from the death squad, away from the structures of injustice that shaped her life. This wasn't a rejection but a relinquishment. She let go of her claim on his life, trusting that God would make a way forward for her son beyond her own context and capacity as a Hebrew mother under occupation. It was a farewell wrought in the furnace of a fierce mother-love.

Jochebed, birth-mother archetype, mother of Moses,

leads us beyond stereotypes of rejection or abandonment. Relinquishment is more often a response born out of harsh and unjust environments. Sometimes the most audacious act of hope, the wildest trust, looks like a baby in a basket.

Jochebed's story isn't the only story in Scripture of a letting go. In the Gospels we see God the Father loosening his grip and allowing his Son to leave his side, entering into the experience of a birth mother, letting go. God knows that to fully belong to humanity, Jesus must leave the divine realm and the rights of heaven.

Imagine Christmas Eve. Jesus is born. Mary pushes him into the world, pondering what his birth means to her as mother, to her family, and maybe to the entire empire. But for now, her son rests in her arms. Joseph enjoys something quite rare for an adoptive father—being on hand when the child comes into the world. This boy is not his and also entirely his all at the same time. This is part of the adoption mystery born that starry night. The joy in that small outpost must have been akin to an adoption homecoming celebration. *Our child is here at last, right where he belongs!*

While the angels are singing and shepherds are hastily making their way to the stable, while the wise men from the East are still a ways off, another One witnesses the story unfold under the midnight canopy. For the first time ever, they're apart. He's just emptied his arms of his Son, entrusting him to Joseph and Mary, but also to humanity.

For the first time, God becomes, in a sense, an onlooker. God sees Jesus cradled in Joseph's arms. For now, he's not the Father. He's the Relinquishing One. And when the angelic choir breaks out in the hallelujah chorus, it's a broken hallelujah, without his Son. It is a moment when we might imagine God at odds with the world, plunged into a solitary grief.

God, who knows what it is to create life and give birth, to brood like a hen over his children and deliver his people like a midwife, now feels bereft and barren. In relinquishing his only child, he feels the pangs of loss every birth mother knows all too well. He enters into the pathos of these women and shares the sorrow only a mother can understand. He's given his Child up for a salvific future, but given him up nonetheless.

When we see that God's experience of family includes relinquishment, it opens the door for us to accept the darker corners of our own family histories, the places where we felt left out or left behind. We can name our own role in relinquishment and speak about the hurt. Family formation can embrace the truth of loss and the practice of lament. This is, after all, not foreign to God's own experience of family.

In lockstep with birth mothers who never forget their relinquished children, God knows that sometimes love looks like letting go. It looks like inviting the wider community to help protect the child you grew in your own belly. It looks like a brave act of trust. Believing this child has a future beyond you, even without you, bespeaks a rugged hope and an undeniable selflessness.

Jesus, biological son of Mary and adopted son of Joseph, is the Adopted One. Relinquishment is part of his own story of incarnation. This isn't only a story about Jesus taking off his divine wardrobe to be clothed in humanity; it's also about confronting the truth of being let go—at least for a time.

All those years in youth-group Bible studies when we poured over Philippians (the always popular, upbeat choice of Paul's letters), this is something I never considered. Quick to talk about how Jesus temporarily emptied himself of divinity, I completely missed the first instance when his Father momentarily orphaned him. As he passed through the heavens en route for Bethlehem, he traveled alone, like any relinquished child awaiting adoption.

Jesus' initial encounter with relinquishment was in the passive voice: he was relinquished. That passive voice precedes every adoption. It's the minor note in even the greatest symphonies of belonging. Even the divine Son knew the pangs of loss and some sensation of rejection.

But then, Jesus also emptied himself. In order to enter

into the human experience with all the vulnerability of a child and all the humility of a servant, he stripped himself of all divine prerogatives. We call this *kenosis,* an emptying, a pouring out of the self. To live a fully human life on earth, he gave up power or some measure of privilege. The self-sacrifice seen in the Incarnation never ceases to amaze me.

One of my professors in college talked about Jesus "abdicating his power." His word choice conjured up the image of a king leaving his throne, walking away from the power, the pomp, and all the privilege of royalty. When a king abdicates, he severs his tie to an inherited position. He may not disown his father, but a distance is created between them when he vacates the seat of power bequeathed to him. I can't help but imagine Jesus stepping away from his Father, accepting the impending change in their relationship.

Jesus relinquished his equality with God; he detached himself from the divine presence of his own Family. In this light, I now see *kenosis* as a kind of letting go, connecting *emptying* and *relinquishing.* But neither should be mistaken for abandonment.

What if living through relinquishment created a capacity within you to more easily let go of whatever stands between you and belonging? Did Jesus' free-fall from his Father's arms allow him to abandon anything standing between him and us? Did leaving the riches and royalty of heaven for our sake prepare him to let go of his own life, for a deeper kind of belonging to us?

Jesus holds deep compassion for all the relinquished ones because he, too, carries this body memory within his own human skin. Whatever his experience of being let go, whether a biting pain or a faint sting, we will never know. But residing somewhere within the body of Christ is the fact of relinquishment and the capacity to comfort us in places where we feel shut out, left out, or pushed out.

Now I find it all the more compelling when I read about Jesus as our high priest, "who has passed through the heavens" and can sympathize with us in these tender places. Jesus passed through the heavens, passed through relinquishment, and remembers what it is to struggle with this part of the human story. His own body holds the memory of being let go and carries the scars of crucifixion—testament to a man relinquished by a Father, by friends, and by the world he inhabited. In solidarity he sits with us in our pain, helping us wait for redemption, because he knows relinquishment does not get the last word.

Our family was enjoying another Burundian summer—the season when we host friends and my husband showcases the lush beauty, athletic drummers, and robust coffee of his homeland. On this balmy evening, friends gathered round the dinner table at a favorite restaurant on the edge of Lake Tanganyika, the laughter thick and spicy like incense.

Justin comes alive around other people, and he could hardly contain the merriment pulsing through his extroverted eight-year-old body. He laughed at all the jokes criss-crossing the table. His eyes darted back and forth like fireflies in the deepening dusk.

I turned my head to order a Fanta, and a mere moment later, noticed his head down in his arms on the crimson tablecloth. As I leaned in, I heard quiet sobs. His sister was chatting on the other side of the table with friends, so I knew she didn't provoke his tears. Nothing discernible had happened, but he was suddenly gripped with sadness.

Rubbing his back in a steady circular motion, I waited for his face to emerge from the pillow of his arms. Slowly it did. "Why did she leave me, Mom? Why didn't she want to keep me?" The heart-crushing words every adoptive mother dreads to hear, but more deeply dreads to answer. Because how do you explain to a small child why his birth mother let him go?

I took his hand in mine and walked with him to a chaise lounge near the small pool. I held him close, his head of tight black curls burrowed into my chest. And I cried with him. We cried together. It wasn't time for words yet, just hot tears. Feelings of rejection sting; how can a little heart weather such sensations?

I remember telling him it was good to cry because it's sad when a mother can't keep her son. It hurts to be left behind. I knew that no amount of reason would fully quell his queries anyway. Our tears mingled on the chaise as the water swallowed the sun, leaving us in the dark.

My son's thoughts still drift to his birth mother. Now that he's older, he's concerned about her poverty. He dreams of finding her and rescuing her from her troubles. He also dreams of her coming to him, inviting him to her house for supper and a game of soccer. But there are moments when he mourns because it's hard for him to believe that letting him go was love, that giving him up meant giving him life. So he questions. He laments. And he hopes.

My daughter, though she is the same age, is only beginning to consider her birth mom, but with a more matter-of-fact curiosity. She wonders what she looked like. Do they share the same sable skin tone, curly eyelashes, and curvy shape? Recently she asked what her birth mom's name was, and though I checked her original Burundian birth certificate, it offered no answer to her question. "It's not fair that I don't even get to know her name, Mom," she said through her tears. So much about relinquishment isn't fair.

I myself was never upset by my relinquishment. I assumed my birth mother was too young to raise a child or maybe too poor to afford a baby. I imagined her going on to finish college and getting married after she arranged for me to be placed in the hands of a couple in waiting, giving us both a chance at a good life. I never harbored any anger or resentment toward her—maybe the imagining helped. In fact, I applauded her choice. Her willingness to carry me to term, to allow me to stretch her body, to twist and turn inside her, altering her appetite (and waist size), made me think she wanted me. She wanted me to know life, even if it couldn't be under her watchful eye. So I never felt shunned—indeed, quite the opposite. She gave me what she could, and it was enough.

I will probably never know what societal pressures weighed on my birth mom. What I do know is that when confronted by the stress and shame of it all, she made a loving choice. Even when cornered with life's worst, she determined that I would live. Even if that meant I couldn't be with her, she would usher me into a better kind of life. That's love. That's guts. And I hope some of that gritty love of my mom's lives in me.

Those of us in the company of the adopted learn early that love can look like relinquishment. This doesn't diminish the sting some of us feel, because the letting go involves hurt and often leaves a bruise on the soul. But the ache can become a locus for another love. Redemption is possible, like a sprout coming from a stump.

Relinquishment is the shadow side of belonging. Letting go and leaving, loosening a tie or losing someone altogether, remind us that orbiting the other side of relationship are the seasons of estrangement, the possibilities of disconnection and the likelihood of loss.

Dear friends of mine raised two sons just a few years apart. One son grew into their exact likeness: he was kind and responsible, became a teacher, and eventually fathered his own children. The other son struggled most of his life with an acute drug addiction that kept him in and out of treatment centers and group homes, in and out of relationship with his parents. Over a long lunch in their backyard one day, they shared with me the searing pain of creating distance between them and their son during the worst of his using days in order to protect the rest of the family and not further enable his addiction. Relinquishing her son, even for a season, flayed my friend's heart open. And the sting of that loss can linger for years. To this day my friends are marked by relinquishment.

Who doesn't know a family torn asunder by divorce? Whether amicable or hostile, the rending does damage. A community created by biology and love and mystery disappears. In its wake come disorientation and confusion. The parents may only intend to relinquish one another, but inevitably they unravel the only community of belonging their children have ever known. Now each one is adrift, unattached in one or more ways from their original center. Each divorce further rends the fabric of belonging as all of us once knew it.

Sometimes we relinquish involuntarily. This is the story of my daughter's birth mother. Because of her station in life, she was exposed to HIV/AIDS. Her poverty prevented her from accessing medication that would have helped her and protected her unborn child from transmission of the disease, which became advanced and attacked both their bodies. And even as she marshaled all her strength to get to the hospital once labor started, her sickness presented complications that couldn't be overcome. She died in childbirth, and my baby girl entered this world with no mother to smile at her arrival, no one to cradle her close. The relinquishment was final—not at all what her mother had envisioned.

Not too much later, my daughter's birth father also succumbed to AIDS, further compounding her loss. As we know, death is an unintended relinquishment visited upon all of us. We are left by those who would have given anything to stay. Diseases, accidents, and all manner of violence rob us of loved ones and catapult us into the arms of relinquishment. We stand by the graveside, grieved, forced to let go before we're ready. We're bereft of belonging.

If we know what it is to belong, then chances are we

know, too, what it is to not belong at all, to feel orphaned by someone or some circumstance. This is the underbelly of belonging that must be named.

From Jochebed to my own birth mother, injustice corners many women and pushes them to let go of their children. And oppressive realities worldwide push people to let go of other elemental things. Not so many years ago, the economic meltdown in the United States forced many of us to let go of our homes in a flurry of foreclosures and short sales. For years before that, farmers across the heartland had been losing land, losing family homesteads and the rhythm of the farming life to agri-business and inequitable trade agreements. More recently, the world watched as nearly 300,000 Burundian refugees left their homes, their land, and their country to find safety elsewhere. A cocktail of predatory economics, political violence, and despotism cornered them into believing that relinquishment was their only or best option.

In her book *Country of My Skull: Guilt, Sorrow, and the Limits of Forgiveness in the New South Africa,* Antjie Krog writes about her experience as a journalist covering the Truth and Reconciliation Commission in the aftermath of apartheid.[1] Black and colored people suffered deep and pervasive abuse under the institutionalized injustice of the apartheid system, a structure that spoke in the dominant language of Afrikaans. Day after day the witnesses would testify, in graphic detail, to the atrocities they were subjected to. The words of oppression were all Afrikaans.

As Krog listened, she realized how much her mother tongue was now wedded to the evils of apartheid. A poet as well as a journalist, she explains how she once wrote poetry in Afrikaans, but now wondered if she ever could again. Her native tongue was so soiled, so disgraced, she felt she could no longer speak it or write it. In her words I hear a woman struggling with the pain of relinquishment, of letting go of her mother tongue, the very language that once marked her cultural belonging.

It seems that any time we move toward belonging, we stumble against relinquishment. Our own relationships might provide the best evidence. It's also visible in the ways we yearn for home—culture, country, and our own plot of land, our own house to anchor us to this place. What emerges? Relinquishment often sits on the other side of justice, revealing what little we have left after injustice steals its dark portion.

One May morning I had the opportunity to talk with Walter Brueggemann, an Old Testament scholar and my theological hero, who was speaking at my alma mater, Fuller Theological Seminary. We both entered the chapel at the same time, well ahead of the others still finishing their coffee in the courtyard. I reminded him who I was and mentioned a mutual friend. Instantly he filled in details with a hearty laugh. He asked if my husband was still in Burundi amid the current political conflict.

Claude is the kind of person whom Brueggemann had been describing in his conference talks: a person committed to justice and active for the sake of neighborhood. While many were fleeing Burundi, Claude determined to stay as long as possible to be with his people. The late-night texts we exchanged between Bujumbura and my guest room in Pasadena confirmed that things were deteriorating fast— armed youth militias, attempts to silence the press, protests producing casualties.

My heightened concern must have been written across my face as I spoke with Brueggemann. He leaned in, looked straight into my eyes, and said, "Your act of justice is to relinquish him." His words, like a whoosh of the Spirit, left my insides trembling with a prophetic rightness.

While Claude labored in and among the collection of protesting neighborhoods to advance the cause of justice, my work was to let him go. This meant not trying to control him or dictate his choices, but to trust that he was actively listening to the Spirit for direction. I disciplined myself to not second-guess his decisions, trusting his discernment and commitment to a more just outcome for Burundi. My contribution to the work of justice was to not impede Claude's pursuit of peace.

In those days I also recognized Claude didn't only or wholly belong to me. He wasn't only my husband or the father to our children. He also belonged to the people of Burundi, to the soil of his childhood and land of his highest hopes. His solidarity with his people emerged as integral to who I knew him to be. He stood with the people of Burundi in the thick of the conflict—and so I stood with them, too. As I relinquished Claude, I found myself more tightly woven into the color-block fabric of Burundi, belonging in a way I never had before.

Deeper still was my realization that Claude belonged to God; I could not have ultimate claim on him. I had known, of course, that he belongs to God in a general sense. But in reality nothing ever trumped my wedding ring, which declared us to belong to one another exclusively. Until people were looking to my husband for the kind of help that could cost him his life, I never experienced a counter-claim. Yet here were his kin needing him to be available and attentive to them, and here was God calling him to center them for the sake of *shalom*. And because Claude belongs most wholly to God, my work was to relinquish my claim and free him to be a person of peace. It was a risk for both of us.

Maybe I was my mother's daughter after all, able to relinquish the love of my life when the situation in Burundi cornered us, entrusting Claude to the hands of God. The kind of solidarity empowered by the Spirit, who binds us all together, wills justice for all his adopted ones.

If we enjoy a robust marriage, a close-knit family, a church rich in fellowship, or a community of committed neighbors, we will inevitably feel the jarring loss when divorce or death comes, the congregation splits, or someone moves away. We will feel the sting when relationships are fractured due to our own imperfect humanity, the many ways we hurt one another and break faith with those we most love. Birth mothers aren't the only ones acquainted with relinquishment. Coming close and letting go, owning and disowning, cleaving and leaving—these are all part of our dance with one another. Relinquishment is part of living in relationship to others— the harder part.

Most disruptive to the larger human narrative of belonging is the relinquishment that results from various forms of injustice. When someone is cornered and coerced to let go of a child, a home, or a homeland, there is reason to name and lament such loss. But we also recognize that relinquishment under such dire circumstances is often the strongest love that can be offered in the moment, when letting go or leaving looks like—and is—love.

Belonging and relinquishment rotate on a shared axis, each taking their turn in the sun. For all the times we're brought close and share the bonds of human communion, there are times we find ourselves estranged or compelled to leave someone behind. We are lost, we are found, and in tandem relinquishment and belonging instruct us and shape our understanding of life together.

The practice of relinquishment offers no guarantees; those in the company of the adopted will testify to that truth. But we can say that letting go is seldom the end of the story. Beyond our sightline, redemption comes, sometimes soon and sometimes slow, but it comes as sure as Sunday.

CHAPTER THREE

Receive

Someone let go, and now someone else steps forward to receive this child. This reception signals the end of waiting, the end of orphanhood, and the beginning of family. Receiving the child will involve, from this day forward, many and varied intentional acts of hospitality that create belonging.

Receiving one another moves beyond meals and bedtime songs as quickly as a child outgrows those tiny Nikes bought by a favorite aunt. Daily practices unfold, and adoptive parents become practitioners of belonging. When we invite the potential of deep difference into our home, we change. Daily hospitality to the other in our midst will likely confront our fears and reveal our ignorance; it will bring someone close and transform *them* into *us*. The stranger will become kin, incarnating the revolutionary hospitality that prophets dreamed of and Jesus incarnated. And it can begin when we receive a child.

My husband and I envisioned a life spent traveling between Burundi and the United States. We imagined international flights, the two of us sitting side by side, reading thick books, undisturbed by anything other than a flight attendant offering us another beverage. Children did not fit into our plan.

A few years into our marriage, we traveled to Burundi for a summer visit. Our path collided with that of a missionary who ran a home for abandoned babies. She insisted I visit. When I did, she led me room by room, introducing me to the babies. Most were sick and recovering from neglect or malnourishment.

She pointed out one boy with chocolate skin and long, banana-shaped dimples, saying he needed a family to adopt him. He was healthy but alone. I hoped someone would adopt him; he looked so small under that soft afro, so ready for love.

Back home that afternoon, Claude and I sipped spicy orange Fanta to cut through the afternoon humidity. Later we slipped under the mosquito net and angled for sleep. *"Will you make room for him?"* The question jarred me awake. Unlike Mother-to-be Mary, I felt unready to answer. This Spirit-breathed question could upend the life my husband and I imagined for ourselves.

I visited the dimpled boy for a string of days turned weeks, trying to imagine us as mother and son. I rocked him under the wispy acacia tree, carried him around the perimeter of the compound, and sang the only lullaby I knew. He grew more comfortable in my arms, but that wasn't answer enough. I lacked adequate imagination. In those weeks, transformation did not come.

The nannies greeted me as "Mother" when I entered the gates, but I didn't feel like anyone's mother. That's what I blurted out to God one hot afternoon as I tried to answer the insistent question. How could I be a mother? "Honestly," I said, "there's so little maternal material to work with here. Your hands, even divine ones, would be fairly tied." And then I heard a whisper: "*Ex nihilo.*" It was a gentle reminder that God had created out of nothing before.

Out of my maternal nothingness, God could create a mother. If I would summon the courage to make room for this boy, I was assured God could create again.

So my son—and my daughter—came as shocking gifts. A year later my husband and I received them in the heavy humidity of a July day surrounded by our Burundian family. They were equal parts eager and curious to meet our adopted children, but like good Africans they would affirm that children—however they arrive—are good gifts from God. This was our first debut as a family, made possible by the imagination and creativity of God.

In the story of Exodus, Bithiah was a woman unready to receive a child. She was the unwed or widowed daughter of Pharaoh—the text leaves the distinction unclear. Reading between the lines of the great Exodus narrative, we sense her unease with the harsh conditions of the Hebrew slaves, her disagreement with her father's death edict for all Hebrew boys. Jewish tradition suggests that she may have gone to the bank of the Nile River for a ritual washing, a cleansing of soul more than body. It was there that the unexpected happened: a boy appeared.

Stuck in the tall reeds in a small basket was a baby boy. Actually, more faithful to the Hebrew language would be the word *ark,* a word the storyteller used to suggest the great flood this boy was escaping, the rising tide of death he would survive (like Noah before him). Bithiah, already knee-deep in the water, drew him out of the river. She knew this boy was under her father's death edict, but she refused to capitulate to that injustice.

The Daughter of Egypt chose to receive the child as her son. The Hebrew woman on the other side of the Nile had also disobeyed the edict, relinquishing this boy into the water, and now Pharaoh's daughter redeemed him from it, playing her part in defying death. It was a creative, courageous act of justice that joined the two women in solidarity on the banks of the Great River.

In a work of collaboration between both sides of the

river, the boy was weaned by his birth mother, Jochebed, and returned to the palace by his sister Miriam before his third birthday. Bithiah took the boy in her arms once again and named him, making the adoption official according to Egyptian protocol. He would be called *Moses*—a word for sonship in her own tongue, lest anyone question her intent. The Hebrew women must have smiled upon hearing the name, which to their ears meant "drawn out," a recognition that she received this gift from them. Bithiah mothered Moses for at least two decades. They did more than share meals at the table. She would have told the growing child stories by day and sung him songs under the light of the moon. She would have been both caregiver and confidant. As he grew older, she arranged for his education, providing him lessons in language, mathematics, ancient wisdom, and archery. Born Hebrew, by her daily care Moses became Egyptian as well. She provided him with everything for life, everything for belonging.

Bithiah received Moses as an unexpected gift. He, in turn, received maternal love from her as he grew and matured. His Egyptian mother, who knew him to be Hebrew, utterly other and different from herself, offered him daily care and unequivocal acceptance. And his dual identities became a pivotal gift that God empowered for a future act of emancipation.

The dual nature of his name foretold his intimate connection to both communities residing on the banks of the Mighty River. Moses—son and survivor, Hebrew and Egyptian, put in and drawn out of the water for the future salvation of many—all the Hebrew slaves and even some Egyptians.

As I tell the story of Moses to my children, it makes me wonder what's in store for them—Burundian and American, relinquished and received, born in extreme poverty and shaped by immense promise.

It is a courageous act for adoptive parents to allow their children to know both of their cultures and engage in the fullness of their own identity. Following the example of Bithiah, we refuse to be afraid of the *other* that comes to us. We will not be afraid of where he comes from or who relinquished him. We will receive him, and them (his kin), with a wide and generous acceptance. If we deny our children the crucial chapters of their story, we might risk hindering them from reaching their full potential in the world. Can you imagine a Moses with no connection to his Hebrew heritage?

Thank God Bithiah made room for the endangered other. She cultivated belonging beyond the brickyards of Hebrew slavery, holding together two cultures and creating a new kind of family bond on the Family Tree. From her small, daring seed of welcome, transformation and liberation blossomed in the sands of the desert.

They all stood in the early morning sun, gathered in clusters round the blue double doors. Mostly mothers with their children, some in shorts and others in their church-best, they waited for the first day of school to begin on this hot August day in Arizona.

Little Emma was in a plaid shirt and a denim skirt, toting her new backpack full of school supplies, so eager to begin second grade. As we approached the school, I noticed one woman with her smart-dressed sons standing off to the side—and I knew why. Her hijab set her apart.

As Emma and I walked closer to the school and to them, I smiled, and we introduced ourselves and initiated some small talk. This was her older son's first day in kindergarten and her first foray into elementary school routines, gaggles of mothers, and all the accompanying protocols. As a veteran, I gave her a few tips for pick-up time later that afternoon. We stood together until the blue doors swung open.

Over the next several days, I kept my eye out for her and her sons, quick to greet them and begin a chat together. I introduced her to Miss Susan, the most kind and astute of the office ladies. I did what I could to make this entire elementary enterprise less strange and frightening.

I soon learned that Tahany was Palestinian by birth and had immigrated with her family as a teenager. Now her husband ran a shop in town while she cared for their two sons. Jamal was quiet, smart, and sweet. Abraham reminded me of Jacob from the Hebrew Bible, the wily younger sibling always grasping the heel of his brother.

On the searing-hot Saturdays of August, Tahany and I would take the kids to air-conditioned restaurants for fast food and indoor playgrounds. We'd sit for hours telling stories and laughing over bottomless cups of soda. While her husband worked across town and mine overseas, we kept one another company. One day she asked me if I'd be the emergency contact for her son, since she had no one else to ask. And some days I'd come to school late to pick up Emma and find her already safe at Tahany's side. We were becoming friends.

The next several months were long, complicated by Tahany's hard pregnancy. Many days I would pick up our kids from school and come to her home. While the kids played, she'd summon enough energy to make me sage tea.

When spring break came, we spent every day at the park on a small knoll under a canopy of trees. We'd spread out our blankets and unfold our chairs. She'd bring the lunch; I'd bring the ice chest full of drinks and snacks—or the other way around. Our kids would run and play for hours like cousins. She'd take Emma down to the pond to feed the ducks, and I'd call to the boys using the Arabic words she had taught me to get their attention.

I remember that on one of those spring days she talked to me about home, about what she had seen in Palestine.

She remembered the Israeli soldiers burning the olive trees. She described standing on the side of the road with others, watching and mourning the smoldering orchard that once belonged to her people. I had read about this in books, but she was reliving her history as she told me, tears falling down her cheeks as I imagine they did back then. We spoke about what it's like to be in land that is occupied, to be considered an other or an outsider. We watched our brown children playing on the monkey bars and wondered together about their future.

At lunchtime the kids ran toward us, landing on the blankets like they were home base. The boys plopped down, panting, as I handed each their favorite juice box. Emma, glistening with sweat and out of breath, rested her head on Tahany's round belly. The two of them giggled as Tahany pulled at her dreads. I recall feeling utterly safe. This was my family.

Years later find us apart. Tahany and her three boys are back in Palestine, and my family is alternately in Burundi and the U.S. But we stay in touch, sharing pictures of our children and marveling at how grown up they are now. We still dream of reunion, this time in Jerusalem. We talk of walking our holy sites together: she will take me to the Dome of the Rock, and I will stand with her in places Jesus stood. But what I most want is to drink sage tea in her home surrounded by my nephews.

Those two years spent with our children sitting around breakfast tables and sharing lunch under the trees, at school pick-up and in hospital rooms, wove us together. I love my generous, kind, Muslim, Palestinian sister. And she accepts me as her white, American, Christ-following sister. We are different, but caught in an embrace that has transformed us both. No longer strangers, but sisters.

Through Tahany I am constantly reminded what is, and is not, required to be related. You can become sisters despite different countries of origin, siblings though different women birthed you. What is necessary for belonging is the habit of showing up for one another, a steadfast presence that endures on good days and bad.

The gesture of invitation indicates our openness to receive the other. We are saying, "There is room for you here." Sometimes this comes with a simple hello and an extended hand; other times it comes with a homecoming celebration and champagne toasts. These are the rituals of welcome.

But once a child is carried across the threshold, once a new friend accepts our invitation to meet for coffee or join us for a family supper, the true work of reception begins. We move from ritual to routine, the unchanging way of welcome which continually affirms that this person is wanted in this place. Our welcome stretches into hospitality—frequent and repeated acts that create belonging.

In the case of adoption, those repeated acts of kindness, comfort, and forgiveness form a family. When I was growing up, I experienced this in myriad ways. It was breakfast with my mom and dad each morning, a lunchbox packed and ready to take to school, a Crock-Pot dinner always on the table (unless it was Friday—which was pizza night). It was clean clothes and homework help and their showing up for dance recitals with flowers for the aspiring ballerina. When I was sick, Mom would nurse me back to health with chicken noodle soup and crackers; when I skinned my knee, Dad was on the ready with Bactine, cotton balls, and a string of silly jokes to make me laugh. When I suffered my first teenage heartbreak, Mom brought two mugs of hot chocolate to my bedroom and got under the covers with me so we could cry together. The three of us learned the practice of apology and how to forgive hurts. Birthday and holiday celebrations, family outings, Saturday chores, and Sunday church all came as consistent and caring hospitality that shaped me into a daughter and them into parents. These same routines of love, kindness, forgiveness, and comfort form me into a mother, my children into a son and a daughter.

Such relationships are developed over time. Offering reliable and steadfast hospitality acts as a formative force revealing something true and lasting between us. If the origin of the word *hospitality* is to be found trustworthy, the initial burden rests squarely on the shoulders of the host. The host opens the door to the guest, the visitor, the stranger, the child—and then anything is possible. Such is the mysterious gift of durable hospitality.

Over time, welcome and committed hospitality pave the path to acceptance. The seasons spent together cull out a place for the other within your life and within you. What was once foreign becomes, somehow, indigenous to the terrain of your heart. You find yourself accepting the unexpected, the previously unimaginable.

Part of the international adoption process requires prospective parents to complete a dauntingly long form where they must check what physical maladies they are or are not willing to accept in a child. This is meant to help the adoption agency find an appropriate match. But I found it to be more like a Lenten intensive, revealing my limitations and prejudices, and laying bare my preferences for comfort over the complications of a special needs child.

I decided to fill out the form based on who I knew my son to be, having met him in Burundi and knowing he was healthy by every measure. A deaf child—no. A mute child— no. A child with AIDS—no. Nonetheless, I cried my way through the form as each ticked box told the truth of who I was. I only wanted to accept a healthy child. I couldn't imagine a life with more complexity or challenge.

But God's imagination is so much wider than my own. It would turn out that my husband and I would bring two babies home. When I was getting to know Justin in Burundi, I met Emma at the same home where he was being cared for. She was in hospice care at the time, her small body riddled with AIDS, all her tests HIV-positive, a girl failing to thrive on every count. I often held her when the nannies took Justin for a bath or a feeding. When Claude and I left for the States, I never thought I'd see her again.

But once I was home, I realized that a connection had sprouted between Emma and me. Maybe it was the time I spent praying for her while she lay in my arms, or how our breathing synced when I carried her round the garden, or how she stared at me with her big brown eyes. Whatever it was, she was planted in me. And when I returned to the States, it was like spring, a field of wildflowers coloring the landscape of my heart. Within those first few months home, I knew that she was my daughter, even if only for a short while.

By the time Claude and I decided to adopt her, the mountains of paperwork had already moved a few steps forward for Justin. I was able to revise our orphan visa request from one child to two. Thankfully, I didn't have to face that dreaded long-form of maladies again. Even so, it would be early July before we'd get the final approval to adopt our children. Within days we were on a plane to bring both our babies home.

It was when we were reunited with Emma and ready for homecoming that we discovered she was deaf in one ear and functionally mute. But by then we loved her, and we brought her home with joy. Stateside, we would learn that she would face speech delays and other challenges. But she was our daughter, and our only thought was to get her the help she needed to thrive.

What I would have rejected on paper, I easily accepted in the flesh, because Emma was not a cluster of daunting health issues but a person already at home with us. In the abstract, so much of her physicality felt foreign and frightening to me. Otherness works that way. Facts disconnected from relationship make us fearful or at least suspect. But when we know someone, when we have welcomed them, the relationship transforms our response.

Burundi is a country comprised of three tribes, the majority Hutu, the traditionally significant Tutsi, and the maligned Batwa. Small in stature, in number, and in local esteem, the Batwa live undocumented on the edges of Burundian society. The first time Claude met someone from this tribe was in 2004.

When our family returned to Burundi a few years later for a long-term stay, Claude reconnected with the Batwa pastor. They became friends slowly, cautiously. One night we hosted the pastor and three of his friends at our home for dinner. We welcomed our new friends with a classic Burundian feast. Stories, jokes, and laughter criss-crossed the table as we had second helpings and the Fantas kept coming. It was a beautiful night.

I didn't notice that one of the women snuck outside to survey the after-dinner dishes. But later in the evening, when we were relaxing on couches, she thanked us for truly accepting them as friends. And then she told us how Batwa people often experience hospitality. People will invite them to a wedding reception, but point them to a separate table in the back of the garden, sometimes even serving them different food. If they're invited around someone's table, they find that the dishes, silverware, and glasses are thrown out afterwards because they're considered contaminated. It's a limited welcome at best.

"But I know you did not throw away our dishes tonight," she said. "Your dishes and ours are piled together in the sink for washing." That cement basin filled with dirty dishes and cups was a picture of acceptance—no distinction between our dishes and theirs, our tribe and theirs.

Hospitality can heal—or hurt. Welcoming each other is not enough; serving each other is not enough. Truly receiving another person includes an embrace of who they are, as they are. We honor what is distinctive and aren't disgraced by differences. Hospitality advances toward acceptance as we push beyond our discomfort, prejudice, and ignorance to let another be at home with us.

A boy walking to school, backpack slung over his shoulder, became a call to prayer. He was black and walking alone. I looked up and down the street, scanning for danger. Even in this suburban neighborhood I felt concern for him, for his mother.

In recent months the nightly news broadcast images of a young black boy in a park gunned down within seconds, of a girl in her bikini grabbed by her dreads and thrown to the ground by uniformed men. Seeing this lone boy on his way to school provoked a protective instinct in me. He would not be hurt on my watch.

As a mother of my own two black beauties, I found myself drawn to the mothers of Trayvon Martin, Michael Brown, Sandra Bland, and Tamir Rice. Over the months of lamenting with these bereft mothers, being attentive to their names and the news, my sensitivity grew into solidarity. Mothers of other black children understood the precarious hand our children have been dealt—or maybe I finally understood.

I knew why they protested, why they feared for the future of their sons and the safety of their daughters. My own white suburban sensibilities recalibrated as I joined these mothers in cries for justice for *all* our children. This is how solidarity works. It's a slow segue from singularity toward community, a conversion of perception and intention. We commit to walk toward a collective goal where we'll be beneficiaries together, or not at all. So now I cannot see a black child without feeling a kinship with his mother.

After adopting a son of the brickyard people, Bithiah wore her royal privilege differently. She spent years faithfully nurturing Moses. As a result, she found herself walking in solidarity with slaves in their struggle for liberation as her adopted son led the way. Jewish tradition holds that Bithiah was a woman of valor who crossed the Red Sea with Moses and the rest of his freed family—the woman who practiced such prophetic hospitality, embraced by the emancipated people.

Bithiah gives us an early glimpse of what the steadfast love, or *hesed*, of God looks like. Like so many adoptive parents, she shows up with uncommon welcome and gives years of durable hospitality to a child. This practiced hospitality opens the door to acceptance and solidarity, which allow us to fully embrace not only a child but a stranger who is in every way unlike us, we think. This is the radical welcome of God.

When the Father relinquished the Son, it was the Child who embodied unprecedented solidarity with humanity as he took on the shape of a baby. Jesus wore our skin, walked our dusty streets, and suffered the injustice too many on earth endure. For thirty-three years he lived as us, among us, exemplifying God's presence and path toward *shalom*. Jesus entered the family of humanity and has never abandoned us since. What reliable solidarity!

This has always been God's way, instructing us to welcome the stranger among us and to care for the widows, orphans, and immigrants. It's why Scripture directs us to leave wheat, grapes, and olives after the harvest—so that the vulnerable ones can partake of a generous gleaning. In the Gospels, we see Jesus welcome street kids into his arms, eat with the outcasts, and envision banquets where the most marginalized are compelled to come. We hear the call in another of the Apostle Paul's letters: "Practice hospitality." Our tradition is clear about the imperative of hospitality as an expression of God's own steadfast love and enduring welcome.

Old Testament scholar Walter Brueggemann defines *hesed* as steadfast love, a reliable solidarity, and includes phrases like "staying power" and "showing up" to indicate the kind of presence you can count on. *Hesed* carries a temporal sense, speaking of duration, an action with stamina. This is the love the prophets so often ascribe to God—a love with staying power that you can count on through thick and thin.

God's hospitality reaches its culmination in *hesed*. The fullest expression of divine welcome is home-coming and home-making, finally knowing that we are beloved and that we belong. When we embody that kind of durable hospitality toward one another, we reflect the *hesed* of God.

When Psalm 23 tells us that "Surely goodness and *hesed* will pursue me all the days of my life," we can feel the durable, enduring nature of God's hospitality at work in this verse. The psalmist continues, "And I will dwell in the house of the LORD forever." God's hospitality both chases us home and is there to receive and welcome us. *Hesed* shapes the very home of God, and Jesus promises there is room enough for all of us.

CHAPTER FOUR

Reciprocate

Adoption stands incomplete until that moment when your child adopts you back. He calls you Mom not because it's your name, but because he's naming who you've become to him. When she's with you, whether you're crossing a street hand in hand or she's jumping into your arms in the pool, her trust is evident.

Every time it happens, attachment is organic and mysterious. The connection between us is strengthened when we reciprocate in whatever measure possible. Our response to hospitality freely given creates a momentum. If we nurture the connection with continual responsiveness toward each other, the flow between us can follow the lead of infinity. That continual loop transforms into a bond, a cord of belonging.

Relational reciprocity is more than a mere exchange or the returning of a favor. Philosophers talk about reciprocal altruism, where you give what you expect another to give you and cultivate a pragmatic goodwill that allows for group formation and cohesion. While the dynamic is similar, adoptive reciprocity burrows deeper, pushing toward family formation. It isn't about what is necessary for the group to survive but what connects humans in transformational ways. This kind of reciprocity has a force all its own—a centrifugal force that pushes outward toward others, including them in our embrace. When we lean in to this kind of reciprocity, it accelerates belonging.

When Emma was eighteen months old, Claude and I brought her home. It felt like we had snatched her from death and disease, from a life defined by a hospice order and lived out in a small orphanage. Her homecoming was a healing.

Months later we sat in her room with its butter-yellow walls, lavender curtains stitched by her grandmother, and a fuzzy green blanket. After a cavalcade of kisses and giggles, she stilled, then looked at me with a hint of a smile. Her eyes reflected an awareness she didn't have words for yet. Gratitude. That's the only way to describe what I witnessed deep in her eyes.

My husband thinks my imagination got the best of me that night. How could she be grateful for a gift she couldn't fully comprehend yet? "You're seeing what you want to see," he cautioned. But my observation stands. She's grateful for her life; she knows she almost lost it.

Gratitude isn't unique to those in the company of the adopted. And not all of us ooze with appreciation. But adopted living can shape something deep in us. We know our life could have turned out otherwise. We could have been left to sickness, resigned to death, or never brought home. But someone decided to welcome us and make room for us at their table.

Such acceptance and hospitality offered daily testify to a life underpinned by grace and gift. I don't take for granted family photos, birthday celebrations, frequent hugs, and nighttime prayers. Even mundane sundries and stern words eventually find appreciation because they point to the truth—I belong here. Against all the biological odds, I found family and a daily table set for me. My adoption invites a silent *Thank you* each night before I succumb to darkness and dreams.

Some of the adopted bring a gritty gratitude as they struggle with the imperfections of parents, siblings, and unknown birth moms. They wrestle and only occasionally see that on the other side of lost, they're found, that on the other side of relinquished, they're redeemed. Maybe we don't know enough about our beginnings to satisfy all our questions, but we hope to know enough to hold on to some goodness. Even a tiny bit of gratitude can be a mustard seed.

Emma is grateful for her life. I'm grateful for the unconditional love my parents continue to offer me, forty-plus years into our adopted life together. And more often than not, my son can express gratitude for our shared life, even as painful questions about his birth mom and relinquishment punctuate his thoughts on adoption. Our daily diet of love tells us we irrevocably belong. I've learned that every family dinner can be a Thanksgiving feast.

Gratitude is the soil where mutuality sprouts. We recognize the goodness of our life, how it's better than it could have been or once was, and we're ready to reciprocate that goodness. This opens the door to a deeper acceptance of our sacrament—they've adopted us and we, in turn, adopt them.

This mutuality, the adoption of one another, cements our connection. My parents adopted me, making me a daughter. My adopting them acknowledges them as parents. It's not only what they offer me, but also what I in turn offer them. They show up with durable hospitality, I respond, they accept me, I more deeply receive them, they walk in solidarity with me, and I honor them every step of the way. This is a snapshot of the reciprocity present in adoption—and in any relationship forged by gestures of belonging. We erase the lines between *yours* and *mine,* making everything *ours.*

This movement of mutuality, where everything is *ours,* is most vividly seen in the Original Family of the Trinity. In this mysterious Three Yet One, we witness a deep relatedness that the early theologians and mystics likened to a dance, a constant movement in and around each other.

The divine dance shaped the internal relationship between Father, Son, and Spirit. The continual giving, deferring, receiving, and sharing strengthened the eternal bond among the Three Persons. But that incessant activity did something else: it generated a momentum that could not be contained within the Three.

The reciprocity of the Trinity spun outward, transforming the space around them. It looked like the creation of the cosmos and the formation of humanity. Indeed, Catholic theologian Leonardo Boff writes that in Genesis humanity is created in the image and likeness of God, revealing traces of the Blessed Trinity.[1] The overflow of Trinity relatedness embraced us, inviting us into a life qualitatively and quantitatively different: eternal, abundant.

To describe the divine reciprocity of the Godhead, the church uses the word *perichoresis*. Parsing the Greek, we see the word suggests a rotating movement. One translation speaks of *choresis* as the choreography of making room; combine that with the prefix, and you see their constant motion of creating room One for Another.

When I was a second-year seminarian, my Greek professor introduced me to Eastern Orthodox icons. It wasn't long before I discovered the pre-eminent work of Andrei Rublev, the Russian iconographer. His icon of the Holy Trinity, gold and luminous, continues to captivate me. The image is also known as *The Hospitality of Abraham,* since it depicts the three visitors who supped with Abraham and Sarah.[2] The three guests are angels who not only accepted Abraham's hospitality but delivered the riotous word that Sarah, childless and well advanced in years, would give birth to a son after all.

They arrived as three men, revealed themselves to be angels, but Rublev saw them as the Three Yet One. It doesn't surprise me that when they were with Abraham and Sarah, life overflowed and broke the hold of barrenness. It seems wherever the Godhead appears, goodness and possibility abound as if even they cannot contain such reciprocal energy.

Discussing this icon in a podcast, Franciscan Catholic priest Richard Rohr pointed out that the three angels sit around the table, each deferring to the others.[3] But one side of the table is vacant. Rohr directed the listeners' attention to the small square on the base of the table portrayed in the image. This icon has been restored more than once since it was painted in the fifteenth century, and what we now know is that scraped away with layers of paint was the residue of glue. It is believed that in an unorthodox move for this medium, Rublev placed a small mirror on the fourth side of the table. When you approached the icon, you would see yourself as the fourth person invited to share in the meal, the fourth person of the Trinity itself. "It is the dynamism of the Three that creates a fourth," Rohr said.

Clearly we are invited into the divine reciprocity of God. The energy that spins within God's Self cannot be limited to the Three; the dance always makes room for another to join them. Belonging is not only about the bonding of one group of people, but a force that reaches out, a magnetism that embraces others. The "infinite outpouring that never stops"[4] becomes our hallmark and family trait. When we extend the sacrament of belonging to others through generous inclusion, we reveal God's divine *perichoresis*-shaped image in us.

Growing up, I always had good friends around me. The only common thread among them might have been their sheer difference from me and from each other. Shannon came from an openly agnostic family at a time when you didn't admit such in public. Thuy was Vietnamese, and Buddhism was the faith tradition of her family. Gil, the only African-American boy in my grade—or on my Christian high school campus—might have been the first boy to ever call me at home just to talk. Terri was the shyest (but perhaps one of the smartest) girls in my class, and I loved walking home from school with her every day. I was also close to Helen,

Chinese and popular and funny. And this is just a random sample of my earliest friends.

High school allowed me to move easily between various groups—band members, cheerleaders, student government leaders, avid readers, and those often holed up in the computer lab. I had as many friends on the football and basketball teams as I had among the self-named "bad boys." While my parents didn't necessarily approve of my knowing the "bad boys" (for fear I might get tempted into trouble), they did appreciate my diverse friends. By contrast, their friends were very white, very Protestant, and very much the same as they were. So no one quite knew where I got my taste for this assortment of friends from various countries, cultures, faiths, and fascinations.

But I wonder if my own adoption-shaped family, possessing an abundance of belonging, spun me outward with arms cast wide. Did the sacramental gestures of an adopted life form me into a net of acceptance for anyone, no matter how different? I cannot definitively say—but I strongly suspect it to be true.

Relational reciprocity bears witness to the truth that there's enough room—in my own heart, at our family table, and certainly in our Father's house. If hospitality is about crossing boundaries to include various people in your home, then reciprocity is about making ample room to accommodate everyone you wish to welcome. The centrifugal force of belonging reaches outward, hooking wide to bring others into a place where they fit. This reciprocity shows us an open vista where there's enough space for all. In true reciprocity I've always sensed a spatial element, an ability to create a large landscape with no limits to the amount of people who could be connected, given enough time and travel miles. I respond to the vision of the Father with plenty of rooms in his celestial home: an open house with ample square footage to welcome others. It sounds utopian, I know. But in my best moments of gratitude I sense a spaciousness that increases my capacity to host people.

Adoptive reciprocity is real, but cannot be assumed. For some there's a natural inclination to respond to family members with an equal measure of hospitality. I've felt this mutuality with my own parents; I've seen it in my own daughter. This mutuality creates a kind of flow that allows us to embrace others with a similar kind of generosity. But unrequited reciprocity is equally real, the chronic pain of trauma making it difficult for a child to respond with appreciation or affection. Sometimes there are periodic pangs of hurt that cripple us from entering into full reciprocity with those who love and care for us. To say this is to recognize that we are still beset by brokenness and dogged by relinquishment. Our ability to respond to others and adopt them back, as it were, can never be taken for granted. For many, reaching back in mutuality toward parents and loved ones is a hard-fought choice, but far from easy.

Reaching out to others, in adoption or other ways, always involves a measure of risk. You don't know if someone will be capable of or interested in responding to your hospitality. Jesus tells a parable about hosting a dinner party without expectations. When you host a party, he says, don't invite your blood relatives, kinsmen, or rich friends because they can invite you in return. Instead, Jesus recommends, invite the poor and the maimed to your feast. When you do this, "you will be blessed, because they cannot repay you."[5] This might be the beatitude of unrequited reciprocity. Here Jesus is unraveling the expectation of reciprocity we harbor when we do something as simple as throw a party. Our tendency is to invite those who have the capacity to return the favor. But imagine if we created a guest list with no expectations. Imagine offering hospitality to someone knowing they most likely won't be able to reciprocate—ever. The Kingdom of God is like that, extending generous invitations with no expectations.

When we adopt a child from a hard place, we know at the outset they might be limited in their capacity to respond to us with unfettered affection. Their early circumstances might have crippled them, preventing them from being able to fully express gratitude for the gift of a home, a family, a future. And yet it is just like God to include them in the feast with no strings attached. This is our invitation—to give our children a feast and not demand a repayment that they cannot offer. Instead, we share in the feast together as best we can on this side of the hurt, on this side of eternity. Then we remember what Jesus says at the end of the parable: there will be repayment at the resurrection of the just. In essence, our participation in God's justice toward a child will be rewarded. God will reciprocate on behalf of those who cannot do so yet. We may die to the joy of reciprocity now, but there will be a resurrection to come.

Jesus tells us there is plenty of room in the Father's house. It is a spacious landscape where all of us can experience homecoming and the joy of reciprocity. We may enjoy a foretaste now, but we are assured full participation in this dynamic of belonging when we arrive at the Father's doorstep at last.

My friend Idelette came of age in South Africa during the imprisonment of Nelson Mandela on Robben Island. She lived in a world of separation: white beaches and black townships, white power and colored people required to carry pass-books, white pastors preaching in Afrikaans and black people worshiping in Xhosa or Zulu. As a white woman, she grew up on the wrong side of justice.

Coming to terms with her own complicity in this system of domination, Idelette determined never to stand over or apart from another person created in God's image. From her metamorphosis she emerged with the capacity to gather others together, no matter what their skin color. Women under the thumb of patriarchy, those most easily victimized, underpaid, and denied power—these especially called out to her. She became a fierce ally for women from Burundi, Uganda, Moldova, and across North America.

Wrestling with the deep pain of separation allowed her to relinquish both shame and superiority. On the far side of struggle, she could receive forgiveness from and find friendship with those once oppressed. The more she embraced others, the more she cleaved to justice, the more she embodied *perichoresis*—and made room for many others to sit on the red couch in her living room and find freedom in belonging at last.

The African word *ubuntu* speaks to the relational dynamic that connects us. I can't remember who first spoke the word to me—Claude with his gentle French accent, or Idelette with her Afrikaans lilt, like a song rising and falling on the crest of a breeze. Perhaps I read it first in Mandela's *Long Walk to Freedom* or Antjie Krog's *Country of My Skull*. But I heard it most simply defined by Desmond Tutu when he said, "A person is a person through other persons."[6]

Idelette teased it out more fully when she told me that if other women are enslaved, then she is not free, because it is only freedom when we are all free. Claude evoked it when he told me that if he did nothing while the Batwa people of Burundi wasted away on the margins of society with no food, no jobs, and no hope for their future, then his own soul would surely wither. They voiced interdependence as only Africans can—using the lexicon of *ubuntu*. Moving from separation to solidarity, from disconnection to alliance, they saw their own humanity irrevocably tied up with the humanity of others.

Many say that an exact translation of *ubuntu* is nearly impossible; it's too big and nuanced and mysterious to be fully pinned down with Western words. *Reciprocity* feels equally elusive. Both words point to a deep connection with others born out of an internal awareness of our humanity and theirs; both speak of undeniable relatedness. Tutu describes *ubuntu* further by saying it recognizes that "we all belong to one family—the human family."[7] Here he echoes the Apostle Paul: we are God's adopted ones. While the church recognizes Jesus as the unique and only-begotten Son of the Father, Paul makes clear that we are all adopted into God's family.[8] We are relatives, related to one another in our shared humanity.

In contrast to the Western notion of Descartes's "I think, therefore I am," the African sensibility is articulated by Tutu: "I am because I belong."[9] Belonging shapes me from the inside out. First I am formed by my family, both my adoptive family and the family I've created with Claude. But the formative work doesn't stop there. From that place of security, I can give more of myself away to others—in my larger community and beyond it. At its most generative, belonging imparts the capacity to shape those around me through inclusion that crosses all boundaries. Like Abraham with his visitors, I make room for another person because *ubuntu* cannot be restrained, and in the end no one will be left out of the feast.

Mama Rose, Claude's mother, hosted her share of impromptu visitors as a pastor's wife in Burundi. She had the habit of saying, "If there's food for four, then there is food for five . . ." as she set down another plate. When another guest knocked at the door, she'd pull out another plate from the wooden cabinet, saying, ". . . and if there's food for five, then there's food for six." It was a generosity that came—and comes still—not from plenty but from security, from assurance in God's abundance and largess. Everyone knows Mama Rose has *ubuntu*.

My husband lives this way still. If we can help ten people with seeds for the planting season, we can help twelve. If we can raise funds for five hundred loans, then surely we can raise enough for a dozen more. If we can afford school fees for our kids, then we have enough to help his brother's kids, too. He's always reaching out because of who Mama Rose shaped him to be—and because of the God whose image he bears.

My husband left the African continent when he married me and we moved into a small apartment in Pasadena. But the adage is true: Africa never left him. Our pillow talk always drifted toward his homeland as he wondered how to embody fidelity from far away. It was during such nights, buried under the covers with legs tangled together, that Amahoro Africa was born.

Amahoro is a potent word in the Bantu language of Kirundi. The word means peace, *shalom*, a full well-being. In Burundi, Claude's mother would greet you by saying "*Amahoro*," and you responded with "*Amahoro*." The exchange continued back and forth until she felt the *amahoro*, the peace, flowing between you. Were you truly bringing her peace? She wouldn't relent with the greeting until she was sure. But Mama Rose wasn't alone in this—all Burundians engage in this traditional greeting. In a country where civil war and tribal strife remain a fresh memory, passing the peace becomes essential. This is the spirit of Amahoro, and the reason why Claude insisted on this word to name our conversations with fellow African leaders. What we desire is peace for Africa, *shalom* that comes only when we join together before God.

The dream was to host a conversation shaped by African sensibilities and African spirituality to address African realities. In his travels with his South African companion, Sean, Claude had noticed that innovative leaders were isolated in their work. They would minister in and out of brothels in Kigali, create communities among street kids in Kampala, and offer tangible care to HIV victims in the Nairobi slums—all this without any support from home churches or denominational structures. Often the bishops and elders laughed at these community practitioners functioning on the fringe. So the Amahoro conversation was birthed for them.

From the beginning, Claude insisted that the Amahoro conversation was not for those who felt supported by their denomination. "If you and your work are embraced by your church, then be grateful and keep at it," he'd say. He wanted to reach out to the misunderstood practitioners.

A few years in, a friend observed that Amahoro Africa, created as a theological and relational space, had become a transformational space.[10] We were Burundian, Ugandan, Congolese, Rwandese, Kenyan, South African—and more. We talked about gospel economics, creation care, reconciliation, and renaissance. Western friends were among our original numbers, but over the years fewer traveled to gather with us. At some point the question was asked: Do we want Western friends to participate in Amahoro?

The resulting discussion explored both the merits and the drawbacks of including Western friends. They came with good intentions, and they brought some influence and even some funding to help our bottom line. But they also brought their tendency to try to control the conversation, to exert their perceived superiority and Western cultural preferences. And some of these very traits reminded African friends of colonial dynamics that had suppressed their voices and their cultures for generations. Amahoro was meant to be a space where African brothers and sisters conversed freely and moved past the colonial experience.

However, our African friends also saw the value our Western friends contributed. So many from Europe and America were eager to learn from African leaders and contribute in a spirit of true friendship. So ultimately we affirmed our Western friends' presence in this conversation. Together we would continue to learn how to heal from hurtful pasts and create new futures. As long as our Western friends engaged in the conversations in non-colonial ways, in a spirit of mutuality and shared exploration, they were welcome. That would keep us on the road of transformation together.

What the Amahoro friends recognized is that the communal goodness generated in our times together couldn't be hoarded. There was room at the table for our Western friends. Inclusion became a hallmark the day we agreed that we belonged to one another. This was good news for me, as one of the few white faces in the room.

Participating in the conversation, I felt like I was standing in front of the Holy Trinity icon once more, looking into the mirror glued to the table they shared. My African brothers and sisters welcomed me in, offering me the relational reciprocity so richly shared among them.

Bart and Linda Tarman are two people who were among the first to teach me what relational reciprocity looks like in practice, in motion. When I lived in Santa Barbara, they invited me to join their family of friends in the mountains one December. There I met a couple that had traveled from Ensenada, Mexico, and another from Guatemala. They included me at their table, and I found myself swept into conversations as if I belonged. Later the Tarmans invited me to come to their home to meet their friends from Nicaragua. Another time it was friends from the Middle East, alongside Democrats and Republicans—all of us sitting around a fireplace sharing in a robust discussion. As I observed this couple, I was struck by their intentional habit of visiting and hosting others, and their inclusion of me in those relational spaces. When I saw how they embodied belonging, it became clear to me that I was expected to do likewise. When you belong, you in turn embrace others and include them in your family, increasing relational reciprocity.

Relational reciprocity in motion looks like a neighborhood church in Texas so rich with kindness and local vitality that they refuse to hoard. Instead, they determine to partner with communities both local and global. They start by partnering with under-resourced schools in the Fifth Ward of Houston. They're among the first to jump into action to assist their neighbors in the wake of heavy rains and flooding. This community of faith also becomes family to Batwa friends, Haitian villages, and churches in Mexico and Uganda. Over the years the church members visit these friends, engaging in joint ventures and shared celebrations. This community erases the distance between us and them, ours and theirs, with a relational generosity that exceeds money. Their practice of reciprocity enables them to belong deeply to both their local neighborhood and communities across the globe. They demonstrate a deep fidelity to God's family.

For those in the company of the adopted, reciprocity is the spiraling deeper in mutual hospitality. We allow belonging to form us by spinning us more tightly together, making us a family. We practice two-way connection, not settling for one-way expressions of care. We move in mutuality with one another. Because the reciprocity at work in our family energizes us, we cultivate belonging not only inside but outside our home. We become sirens of belonging in our schools, churches, and workplaces. This is where adoptive goodness turns outward—we are blessed to be a blessing to others.

True belonging is part of the divine dance that always makes room for others at God's table. When we belong well to others, that connection cannot be contained. The goodness within spins us out and creates our capacity to include others in a spirit of *ubuntu*. Desmond Tutu says that *ubuntu* is a deeply compelling force capable of removing barriers between us. It is a process, he says, like a cosmic embrace where "None is an outsider, all are insiders, all belong."[11]

CHAPTER FIVE

Redeem

When I lived in Santa Barbara, my friends Bart and Linda Tarman introduced me to their closest friends visiting from Guatemala, Don Salomon and Doña Mery Hernandez. Throughout the evening the couples spoke in rapid-fire Spanish punctuated by bursts of laughter—and no amount of translation could completely unlock the humor of those inside jokes shaped over years of friendship.

Bart and Linda had traveled often to the village where Don Salomon and Doña Mery lived, and almost as frequently the Hernandezes had come to stay with them in California. Don Salomon's English got better; Bart learned Spanish. They were always talking about Jesus, always talking about accompanying the poor.[1] Think of all the things weathered over twenty-plus years of living, the sweet and the bitter in turn, and imagine these four friends faithfully showing up for all of it. A patina emerged as they raised kids, shared friends, and shaped communities together.

Early in their friendship, the four climbed the greened slopes of Guatemala. Don Salomon shared his heavy heart for the people of this mountain community. They needed doctors. Together with his American *compañeros*, he dreamed of a clinic that would have one bed and one doctor, and that it would be the one place people could get to for emergency medical treatment. Together, they held this dream.

Years later they still travel between their countries and share too many inside jokes to count. Both the Hernandez children have medical degrees. The Tarman clan speaks fluent Spanish and knows Guatemala like a second homeland. Together these friends founded the Westmont Bethel Hospital in San Miguel Petapa. Not one but eleven beds are available for preventative, routine, and emergency care for this small community.

The health care made available to this otherwise impoverished village is a testimony to the deep fidelity of these friends. Don Salomon and Doña Mery, Bart and Linda show me that the redemptive work of *hesed*, steadfast love and reliable solidarity, can look like eleven hospital beds, doctors, nurses, a surgical suite, and hope for redeemed bodies.

The first time I held Emma in Burundi, I was sitting on the twin bed that doubled as a couch. The nanny handed me a baby girl swollen with sickness and loosely swaddled in a thin blanket. I sat with her on my lap, listening to her labored breathing. This was the little girl in hospice care, expected to die within the next few weeks.

Emma struggled for each breath, her unflinching eyes fixed on mine. I put my hand on her chest and watched my fingers rise and fall with her inhale, her exhale. I prayed for her to know a life outside this compound, a life with family and parks and health outside these walls. I cradled her until another nanny returned for her.

Months later I learned that none of the nannies wanted to touch Emma. These rural women weren't trained nurses schooled in neonatal care or contagious disease transmission. They knew her mother had died of AIDS and guessed, rightly, that Emma's symptoms were connected to that same disease.

Claude and I left Burundi intending to adopt only Justin. I said farewell to Emma, assuming we'd never meet again. Once back in the States, my husband and I began the long adoption process for our baby boy. We spoke regularly with the American missionary running the center in Burundi to get necessary paperwork in order and check up on Justin's growth while we were apart.

During one such call on a November night, after we finished our business talk, the missionary shared news about Justin. Then, unprompted, she told me about Emma and her resilience, how she was still fighting to live and showing some slight improvement. I almost missed her words entirely because I heard another Voice, as if on another frequency, say, *"She's yours, too."* I knew the Voice; I recognized the timbre and the invitation.

This time there was no question, just a simple declaration: *"Yes, she's my girl."* If there was room for one child in our home, then certainly there was room for two.

I knew Emma would come home sick. I had no illusions that an American homecoming would be a panacea. What I believed was that her remaining months, maybe years, would be filled with mother love. Sickness wouldn't bar her from belonging in a family. I began praying daily for her health as the adoption process lumbered on. She kept testing positive for the virus; I kept buying her brightly colored dresses.

Hosannas echoed across the auditorium that Sunday morning in January when I heard the Voice intrude once more, this time with an instruction: *"Pray for her like you pray for Justin. I'm healing her."* This wasn't what I had expected. Standing amid the congregation, singing hosanna, a mustard-seed faith eluded me. I kept the promise to myself.

While my prayers changed, Emma's test results didn't. And come July, when I boarded the plane bound for Burundi to reunite with Claude and my babies, now approved for orphan visas, I was nauseous. I had no medical visa, no mustard-seed faith, and no plan B. The last call from Claude before I traded a boarding pass for an aisle seat confirmed what I had feared—she was still testing positive. It was a long thirty-four hours in transit, moving closer to her, but also closer to the fact that I had misunderstood God.

Once in Burundi, Claude and I took full custody of our children and were finally a family. Our first task: get medical approval from a U.S.-approved doctor for both the babies. This was all that stood between Emma and homecoming. We sat in the doctor's office waiting our turn for tandem exams for our children.

I remember hoisting Emma onto my hip and taking the long walk from the pale green waiting area into the exam room. She sat on my lap and stretched out her arm for the nurse. She giggled, unfazed. I tried to smile back and exert an air of calm through my tears. Everything hinged on Friday, Saturday, and Sunday—that's what I nicknamed those three blood vials.

As if on cue, we got a call on the third day. Claude was told to bring the babies back to the medical office for some necessary vaccines and the medical approvals. Stunned and still unsure, he had the nurse read off all the test results until he heard her say, "HIV-negative." And just like that, my daughter's body was redeemed.

I've been told that healing doesn't happen anymore— or it never did. Several people have explained to me that

Emma's birth mother's antibodies were in her system for seventeen months, resulting in positive blood tests. But when those antibodies finally flushed out of her system, conveniently before that critical blood draw, her true negative status was revealed.

"See," they say, "no miracle." But in every measurable way my daughter was sick. And now she's my Sunday girl, dancing and singing hallelujah.

The bruised ones, whether in Guatemala or Burundi, remind us of our world riddled with brokenness. Our bodies know it; our communities know it. We long for a wholeness to heal us all. Put another way, we hunger for God's original *shalom*. We remember Eden, where we last stood naked and unafraid, where wholeness permeated the garden paths. Then comes the brokenness between Adam and Eve, between Cain and Abel, even between humanity and the earth. We join a story rife with the sickness and ravaged relationships of a fractured world. My own relinquishment as an adopted daughter brings the brokenness close. But I'm learning that when the relinquished call, redemption often responds.

Brokenness opened the door to redemptive work in my life. By the strength of one mother, I was born despite the odds towering against her. Another mother, saddled with infertility, imagined a family that included me. Both these women demonstrated how brokenness can give way to wholeness. They taught me I could be relinquished in love and redeemed by love. I learned I could trust redemption to come in this world.

Every Adoption Day my mother made her minty grasshopper pie with a chocolate cookie crust. She brought it to the table as our reminder that redemption happens. Each slice tasted like a second chance—a fresh start for my first mother, a chance at family for my adoptive parents, and a possible home for me. All the years of adopted living redeemed something in each of us. Throughout years of celebration and everyday living, my roots spiraled downward, entwined around something more primordial and *good*. Redemptive energy seeped into my marrow, burrowed into the depths of my soul. This was the source of my confidence in God, my trust in the goodness of others, and the taproot for all my utopian hopes for the world.

Friends describe my outlook as optimistic to the point of being unrealistic. I understand their suspicions of my redemptive worldview. Not every wrong is made right, not every hurt healed this side of eternity. Indeed, it is a slow kingdom coming.[2] And yet I cannot shake my redemptive sensibilities. Experiencing a fractured friendship, seeing a broken and besieged community, or hearing news of disenfranchised people still sends me searching for redemption. Hope for reconciled relationships and restored communities is in my blood. My eyes are trained to see redemption—where it is present and where it is needed. My body tells me this is natural. The redemption of all things is woven throughout Scripture but also threaded through my own experience. It informs my expectation to witness God actively restoring all things.

My story could have been otherwise, but my parents redeemed me through adoption. My son could still be in an orphanage. My daughter could have perished under the weight of sickness or be surviving in silence without a hearing aid. But rescue came to us. I hesitate to use the language of rescue, to cast adoptive parents as saviors, because I know that can be problematic. Some don't experience adoption as redemptive but rather as a reminder of an original loss. Adoptive parents aren't superheroes or saints. The legitimate words of caution and real complications that are part of adoption give me pause. And yet redemption, whenever it happens, must be named.

There are many redemptions. One family member forgives another, and their connection revives over time. A friend lost to addiction comes clean—and comes home. A widower is surprised by winter love, a single professional finds community as she engages in local activism, a single parent discovers neighbors who can babysit, linger on the porch together, and watch the kids play and share family meals. A family stays in their home after a foreclosure order is thwarted. A cancer patient, surrounded by doctors, nurses, and best friends, rings the bell declaring the end of chemo treatment and the dawn of remission. It is good to name all the ways in which we are saved—redeemed—by belonging one to another.

In the biblical narrative of the book of Ruth, we're drawn into the story of two women struggling to survive on the margins of Jewish society. The story begins with an ecological disaster—there's famine in Bethlehem. Naomi and her family decide to immigrate to Moab, where the land is fertile and resources are rich. She comes to the new land in fullness, boasting of a husband and two sons. But within a short time we learn that her husband dies.

Her sons take Moabite wives. And yet in ten years' time, both Naomi's sons die. Having lost everyone dear to her, Naomi decides to return to Bethlehem. She recognizes that the Moabite wives lived in *hesed* toward her and her sons. Indeed, we hear her pray aloud for God's continued *hesed* toward the young women. When the time comes for her to leave Moab, she releases Ruth and Orpah from any obligation to join her and readies herself to return to her homeland empty and bitter. But she does not return *alone*.

Insisting she return with Naomi to Bethlehem, Ruth speaks those well-known words of belonging: "Where you go, I will go. And where you stay, I will stay. Your people will be my people, and your God, my God."[3] It's unclear how much Ruth knew about the God of Israel, but it's clear that the years she had known Naomi had birthed a deep fidelity that persuaded Ruth to relinquish her own homeland in favor of her mother-in-law. We begin to see Ruth emerge as the embodiment of human *hesed,* steadfast loyalty, and enduring hospitality, qualities usually associated only with God.

It's odd to see a Moabite—the eternal outsider, according to the Jews—so deeply aligned with the character of God. But there she stands, the woman of valor and *hesed*, according to Scripture.[4] Ruth is loyal in ways no one expects her to be. Society doesn't require her to cross borders and help provide for her bereft mother-in-law. Even Naomi tries to discourage her at first. The story describes Naomi as bitter, broken-hearted, too waylaid by grief to show even a mite of gratitude for Ruth's companionship and care. But Ruth isn't looking for affirmation; she's preoccupied with providing for this woman by gleaning fields meant for widows, immigrants, and other vulnerable ones.

At this point in the story of Ruth and Naomi, we witness a redemptive solidarity. It illustrates the redeeming that occurs in the context of relationships over time. In many of the narratives around me, I can see shades of Ruth. I see her in my dear friend Jessica, an adoptive mother to her sweet Chinese-born daughter. Night after night she shows up to help her daughter process heavy emotions of loss that often approach at bedtime. And she is there morning after morning, offering new mercies that move her baby girl toward wholeness. With humor and hospitality, despite frustration and exhaustion, she mothers her daughter through grief and into belonging. She's not looking for anyone's approval or applause; she's only interested in the welfare of her daughter. And what I see in Naomi, I also see in Jessica's young daughter: hints of unrequited reciprocity. Due to deep trauma caused by unspeakable loss, they cannot reciprocate in redemptive ways—yet. But redemption is still at work, bringing a greater wholeness.

Another reflection of the story of Ruth and redemptive care is visible in my friend Janelle. I met Rick and Janelle in a neighborhood Bible study group when we first moved to Arizona. Years later, Janelle tends to her husband, who is both physically and mentally declining in his advanced age. She exhibits fidelity and tenderness amid the storm of Alzheimer's. She gleans goodness where she can to nourish her husband and sustain their love. Each day, much like Ruth, she lives out her insistence on *hesed*. It is redemption in action.

My friends show me how *hesed* is an unrelenting fidelity to the people in your life. They also are the hands of redemption. What is more redemptive than helping an orphan find her home? Or savoring companionship amid the disorientation of dementia? These friends stand alongside the couples caring for the medical needs of a community in Guatemala, long-term relationships creating redemptive possibilities like those we see between the two women in the biblical story. Have no doubt: Our interconnectedness breeds redemption.

Redemption isn't synonymous with physical healing. Not all bodies are healed; my family knows that well. After I was adopted, almost as soon as I came home, my mother began to suffer vertigo attacks and other symptoms that confined her to bed for days at a time. Her undiagnosed condition continued long enough to derail my parents' hopes of adopting a brother for me. There were so many doctors, medicines, and unanswered questions for much of my childhood. I remember every plan (going to Disneyland or Bloom's Ice Cream Parlor, playing Boggle together after school) came with a caveat: *As long as I feel okay.* I grew up knowing that bodies are precarious, my mother's most of all.

My mother prayed faithfully for a complete healing. She was anointed with holy oil and slain in the Spirit. She participated in prayer meetings and healing prayer, believing her healing would come. She attended healing services and heard holy men prophesy over her, promising a healing that never arrived. For decades she held out hope—she does still. It's exhausting for her and for those of us who love her. But she remains hungry for healing even if, as she now admits, it comes on the other side of this life.

When my appetite for redemption confronts my mother's chronic illness, I feel the tension of what remains incomplete. I remember that we live between the now and the not yet of God's Kingdom, in a place where we not only see dimly but experience healing too infrequently. Redemption is always a mystery, never a formula. But this tension stokes a fire in me; it is continual fuel for my hunger to see her healed.

The tugging tension returns when I hear that Amber's son hasn't gained a single ounce since his last weigh-in, and another road trip to Little Rock brings no answers. There's still no cure for Alzheimer's. There aren't enough clinics in Guatemala. These facts remind me of the fracture we endure on earth, and that incessant tension between health and disease, peace and war, life and death. We feel it in our bones, in our souls. He died on Friday and was resurrected on Sunday.

The redeemed carry this ache for all that is unhealed. All the more reason to recognize physical redemptions when they do occur—to see that redeeming happens in part now, but one day, in full.

In his letter to the Romans, Paul spoke of the very real tension between the now and the not yet of God's Kingdom. We stand alongside creation, he said, together groaning and waiting for "our adoption, for the redemption of our bodies."[5] Created and then cursed, together we will know restoration from the ground up. The bond between land and lives threads from the Torah through the prophets and is woven into the theology of Paul. Those who best understand the connection between soil and soul have a head start when it comes to the practice of redemption on this side of eternity.

Boaz, the third character in the book of Ruth, is a man rooted in Bethlehem in the land of Judah. Like Naomi's husband, he has ancestral holdings in Bethlehem. His fields appear well-tended and fertile, boasting abundant crops of barley and wheat. After the harvest, Ruth comes to his fields to glean what is left over. As a foreigner without a husband, she knows this is her only way to provide food for herself and Naomi. When Boaz notices her in the fields, he asks after her and learns that she is a good woman caring for her mother-in-law. So he instructs his workers to protect her and even give her an extra portion of grain to take home at the end of the day.

The fact that Boaz directs his workers to deliberately leave portions of the field untouched so there will be ample opportunity for people to glean tells us more about his character. He lives and works in accordance with laws in both

Leviticus and Deuteronomy, mindful of the most vulnerable in his community. He understands his duty to them.

This good man is a Jubilee practitioner. He understands that the land belongs to God and the community, that it's to be cared for season to season and someday to be redeemed from toil. Boaz cultivates the land in such a way that the post-famine economy thrives, as do the families on it. No one listening to the story of Ruth should be surprised to learn that he is a redeemer who is in line to rescue her from the margins of society. We watch as these three converge: Naomi, the widow repatriating to Bethlehem; Ruth, the Moabite immigrating there; and Boaz, the man who stayed rooted in his homeland, committed to the earth.

In the book of Ruth, and in the intertwined story of these three characters, what is at stake is full-scale redemption of land, lives, and a family legacy. Ruth and Naomi will remain on the edge of community life unless someone redeems them. This responsibility usually falls to a male family member able to purchase the land and keep it in the family and maybe even marry the young widow to offer her a place and protection in the community. Boaz isn't the first in line to save the family farm—there's another kinsman redeemer more closely related. Boaz isn't the most likely candidate to become Ruth's husband, either. A brother is the only one expected to perform that function. But with no brother and only an unwilling cousin on the horizon, Boaz goes to great lengths to secure the ancestral land for Naomi. He defies so-cial expectations by marrying Ruth and ensuring her status within her adopted homeland. He incarnates Jubilee, even returning the family name to the genealogy of Israel, with Ruth's name in the direct line of Jesus—such good news.

The prophet Isaiah speaks of a dry land that comes to life with multiple water sources—rivers, fountains, and pools of fresh water transforming the parched earth. He tells of a variety of fruit trees that will populate the once-barren land of Judah. He paints a picture of useless and untended earth redeemed. The transformation of the land rescues the people who depend on it for their livelihood. When land is redeemed, so are those who live on it. When Boaz cares for the land as God commands, women like Ruth and Naomi partake in redemption. And when Ruth gives birth to their son, Boaz has redeemed the land for another family. Biblical wisdom tells us that land and family are intimately interconnected.

When we first met our Batwa friends, they lived on a strip of land along a pock-marked road that cut through the Burundian countryside. The government (claiming the land for a cemetery) moved them just days later. The seventy Batwa families were relocated to a more dire parcel, far removed from the road (so they wouldn't be seen, the soldiers said).

Nothing ever grew in this place. A dirty water source was a five-hour walk—one way. The hills lay out across the land like naked breasts, brown and flattened by hardship.

Still, the call of Isaiah's song would not leave us. Over a couple of years we secured land deeds and water rights, then dug deep wells powered by solar hydraulics. The community decided on an ample number of wells to share with their neighbors. Every day the children showered themselves into a lustrous brown. And gradually those on that land became hydrated and energized. After learning about irrigation and practicing the agricultural traditions of their grandparents, they began to plant seeds and dared to hope. And then came pineapples like golden blossoms, sweet potatoes nestled in the darkening soil till harvest, so many shallots that I was once handed a bouquet of them on a Saturday morning visit. The land blushed green—and it was as if Isaiah sang with us. Land and lives are still transformed today. I've seen it with my very own eyes.

But I and many others are hungry for more redemption. My ancestors stole land, and I ache for my government to act in good faith at last and honor hundreds of treaties with our First Nations people. We stole men and women from their homeland, and I want to dare to imagine what redemptive reparations might look like on our shared soil. I want to see townships torn down in favor of good housing and land rights for my South African friends. I want to see walls crumble, roads open, and Palestinians return home. I want refugees to find some kind of redemptive goodness in resettlement among hospitable neighbors like Boaz. I want to witness the meek inheriting the earth, because only then will our belonging be complete—when we are all at home.

Naomi came home from Moab empty, with a grief so heavy it felt permanent. She told everyone to call her *Bitterness* from then on.

It took time before the sorrow cracked open enough for a spark to alight. It took time for Naomi to notice the kindness of Boaz to her daughter-in-law and to recognize the faithfulness of Ruth in the fields, providing for them both. Still more time—nearly two harvest cycles—before her pain unclenched its fist and allowed her to hope, to participate in life again. "Don't you want a home of your own?" she asked Ruth. "Oh, look! Boaz is winnowing the barley tonight," she observed, eyebrow slightly raised.

And the waters under the dry land began to move. Naomi hatched a plan to bring Ruth and Boaz together. She gave Ruth a string of instructions about making herself known to him. Naomi wasn't too old to remember the customs of wooing. And so she schemed.

Having weathered much of life's worst—famine, migration, loss of spouse and children, loss of protectors and providers, repatriation and the misery of grief—she expected *only* bitterness. In such a state, no one—least of all her—expected any good on the horizon. *Bitterness* was her name and her lot. Until she dared to imagine a redeemer for Ruth, for herself.

Ruth's story is much more than a romance; it's about the anatomy of redemption. Ruth is redeemed from outsider to insider, woven into the very genealogy of King David.[6] And Naomi herself, at last, is redeemed. Boaz has bought her husband's land, restoring her to the community, and Boaz and Ruth have a son, gifting her with kin. At the end of the story she stands as she did at the beginning: full.

Against all the odds, Naomi returned to her home and found hope. Ruth embraced a new homeland and found belonging. Boaz shared his home and land and created a place of belonging. And God, though curiously unnamed in the story, worked redemption through the human hands of *hesed*. Together they cultivated belonging in this landscape.

The afternoon sun cut low across the living room as Emma and I sat on the couch. At age eleven, she was asking to hear another part of her story: What happened to her birth mom?

I told her that her first mom carried a disease in her blood, one that made her very sick. But at the same time she carried life—Emma's life. The day Emma was born, both life and death had their say. We cried together as I confirmed her growing suspicion: her mother died of AIDS while giving birth to her.

To help Emma cope with this part of her story, I began a ritual with her. When she felt sad or angry about her mother's death, we lit a red candle together. More often, though, she'd bring me the yellow candle. When I'd strike the match, Emma would say "Thank you" to her birth mom for getting to the hospital in time for her to be born, for using her final burst of energy for her.

On my nightstand at the time of one candle lighting was James Cone's *God of the Oppressed*. On the cover is a graphic sketch of Christ crucified, hanging on the cross, body gaunt and bent. My daughter, seeing the image, asked if Jesus really died.

"Yes," I nodded. Then I added, "Three days later God raised him from the dead." I anticipated an Easter smile, but her brow furrowed further.

"Why doesn't God raise my birth mother?" Here was the resurrection question I wasn't ready to answer.

What do we do between the first resurrection and all the others? For my daughter, this isn't a theoretical question. She doesn't do "theoretical." She wants to know why God can redeem her body, but not her mother's.

Two of Emma's Burundian uncles died of cancer; both her parents died of AIDS. My two paternal uncles died of heart failure. For the past fifty years my own mother has lived with a chronic illness unabated by healing. Our family, so full of redemption, yearns for more. We live between the now and the not yet of resurrection.

I imagine Naomi would have understood my daughter's question. Have they both found belonging and tasted redemption? Yes. But even in her new chapter of redemption alongside Ruth and Boaz, Naomi lived with the loss of her husband and the wish to see her sons again. How could it be otherwise?

Relinquishment and redemption, death and resurrection always function in tension.

Redemption doesn't erase loss; it remembers it. Boaz said as much when he spoke of his marriage to Ruth as a way to "raise up the name of the dead."[7] Strictly speaking, he was addressing land redemption and the ancestral name. The wider sense is of a true redeeming that creates space to remember those lost to us, whether by death, relinquishment, or some other kind of departure. We don't move on from them or forget them; rather, we embrace them in the new life we've found.

This kind of redemption makes room for birth mothers. We miss them even as we love our adoptive moms, as my son says. We can hold difficult truths about them and wrestle with hard questions, all the while grateful for their gift of life to us—as my daughter articulates. We can hope for the best for them, as I do, longing for their own redemption on the far side of relinquishment.

It's important to know what Naomi knows: There are many potential redeemers in our story. When Naomi first learns of Boaz and his kindness toward Ruth in the fields, she says to Ruth, ". . . he is one of our redeemers."[8] In context she likely means he is in the line of potential kinsman redeemers. What she knows is this: There are others, maybe many others, who can step into that redemptive role.

When we think of redemption, our inclination is to rush to its zenith: Jesus, the descendant of Ruth and Boaz. But this runs the risk of missing all the other redeemers who contribute to the stories of Scripture. They are models for us as we consider relational redemption. When we witness Bithiah and Queen Esther, Moses and Joseph, the adoptive father of Jesus, we see how we participate in the redeeming work here on earth.

How do we recognize the redeemers in our life, as Naomi did? Do we have eyes to see those with redemptive capacity? In my own story, I've come to see the Holy Family Adoption Agency and the vowed women of the Sisters of Social Service as redeemers. Together these organizations and their dedicated workers facilitated my relinquishment, foster care, and eventual redemption as an adopted daughter. I

look at the yellowed documents with their careful penman-
ship, their exact signatures, and consider each appointment
kept, document double-checked, and decision made on my
behalf. They moved through a *shalom* structure to ensure I
found a home, a family where I would belong.

Janelle, the friend I mentioned earlier, is another practitioner of redemption. Every Monday morning we meet
for coffee. We talk about books we're reading, ideas we're
chasing, and all the peculiarities of life that week. In a town
where I often feel socially marooned, she is my lifeline more
than the caffeine in my cup. Nearly my mother's age, she has
been the maternal presence I've needed to weather some
arid times. She shows up, she calls, she checks the mail when
I'm overseas. These might seem like small things, but she's
helped hold me together through chaotic times. She weaves
redemption into my soul. And I recognize her as one of the
redeemers in my life.

My mother is a redeemer in her own family. During
more than twenty years of functional estrangement from
her three sisters, she never entirely lost hope that they'd
one day reconcile and enjoy each other's company again.
She would confess her efforts weren't perfect, but always
prayerful. Her stubbornness paid off, and at long last, there
was a breakthrough that triggered a domino effect of reconciliation among these four women. Now they take trips to
Hawaii together, celebrate the baptism of granddaughters,

and exchange texts as quickly as their fingers can fly. Thank God for those with hearts able to hold out hope over the lean years, for they will taste redemption.

There are many redemptions and many redeemers. This is part of the anatomy of belonging, the ways in which we participate in saving one another by showing up, walking in solidarity, and never losing hope. This is what Naomi knew about redemption: It may take an entire village and even a Moabite woman to redeem you, and you ought not to miss out on playing your part as either redeemer or redeemed. In the company of the adopted, we are never too far removed from the work of redemption. And as adopted ones, we share in these redemption songs.

CHAPTER SIX

Repair

War, death, and disease rend the world. Injustice tears at the fabric of neighborhoods, making relinquishment the best but most heart-wrenching choice under bad circumstances and leaving behind orphans, families at risk, people side-lined with no support system or sign of hope. Adoption is one way we dare to stitch the world back together. It offers a needle and thread to begin the mending. We cannot mend all the wounds, gather all the fragments scattered about war zones and orphanages and underserved neighborhoods—but we do what we can with each stitch.

The Jewish community speaks of *tikkun olam,* or "repair of the world."[1] It isn't a biblical term per se, though it is deeply congruent with the imperatives of Scripture. It suggests much of what Scripture says outright about God's restoration project—that we are to repair the streets where people live, to become reconcilers between factions, and to reclaim the original *shalom* of Eden. Irwin, a rabbi and a gentleman, tells me that *tikkun olam* is the recognition that we each do small things toward the healing of our society. Each of us makes individual contributions toward the collective work of justice.

Every time a family chooses to enfold, to adopt a child, or someone reaches out in friendship to someone unlike himself or herself, they are re-making the world, making a single stitch toward wholeness. Every stitch is both a personal and a political statement about the fracture-making ways of the world. Our small gestures insist that everyone belongs and that the structures of the world must be calibrated toward inclusion.

One June morning Claude stood among thirty Batwa families on the edge of a pristine plot. For landless people, this was like crossing into the Promised Land. But they had taken only a few steps into their new home when angry neighbors met them, vowing to run them out. The hostility was tribal, the Hutu and Tutsi neighbors saying that the Batwa would poison the land.

The thirty Batwa families determined to "embarrass the neighbors with their love," as the Burundian adage says. When the Hutus falsely accused them of stealing cabbages, the families gave them twice as many cabbages in return. When the Tutsis stole their carrots out of the ground days before harvest, the families didn't seek revenge but gave them potatoes, too. Each week the families would sit with Claude and tell him these stories, and then they would dream out loud about a future in which they would all be friends, all have ample food, and all live in peace throughout the mountains of Matara.

Our Batwa families had a prime location: land right on the main road with easy access to the elementary school, the local market, and the little health clinic run by the Catholic nuns. For their Hutu and Tutsi neighbors, the most direct route to these resources was a rutted footpath along the Batwa property line. The neighbors tried to avoid touching the Batwa land, but it wasn't easy, given the logistics of the area. The Batwa noticed how hard the coming and going was for their neighbors. They also recognized what a hardship it was that no truck could get back to their communities to deliver bags of seed, or build a home or repair one. That's when they came up with a possible solution brimming with *tikkun olam*.

During the next weekly meeting with Claude, the Batwa leaders asked if they could gift the land on the periphery of their property line to the larger community for the creation of a public road for their neighbors. This project would involve the Batwa ceding about 10 percent of their land for the welfare of their enemies. Their only stipulation? That their neighbors had to build the road with them. Applauding their creative act of love, Claude green-lit the project.

Over the next six months, Hutu, Tutsi, and Batwa neighbors worked together every Saturday morning to build a car-worthy road right to their doorstep. At first, the mornings were quiet. The neighbors needed the road but begrudged the givers and tried to keep to themselves. But over time the animosity began to unravel. The men came with their tools and their sense of humor, and they began laughing and working in mixed groups. Working together, they became friends. And when the road was finally done six months later, they walked it together in peace.

Now, six years later, the mountains of Matara are a transformed place. The three tribes share the extra produce from their harvests with one another; they work shoulder to shoulder in the fields; they walk to the market together on Mondays and Wednesdays. Their children go to the same school, rewriting the old stories of bullying and discrimination. The verdant fields of cassava and sweet potatoes, the chartreuse rows of cabbage, the robust tea bushes flanking the land—all exemplify the abundant plantations of *shalom* that Ezekiel the prophet once imagined.[2]

True, the Batwa families aren't perfect. They still squabble with one another and need elders to arbitrate disputes. Occasionally one will take more than his fair share and run away until he can face the community again. And the community isn't exempt from bossy leaders and competing ideas about the common good. But these friends are, nonetheless, on the road toward peace.

And this is their Promised Land. The families now boast of food security. Their children have a bright future. They are at peace with their neighbors and even the leaders in the community at large. They embody *tikkun olam,* having offered the first stitch of *shalom* in their community, opening the way for deep repair across the region.

Shalom is a wide word. It carries the meaning of peace, well-being, and wholeness. The lush Garden of Eden gives us a glimpse of the original *shalom,* where creation and humanity support each other, where we witness abundance, security, and freedom as the world begins the way God intends.

While *shalom* may refer to an individual's quality of life, most often it refers to a communal practice that brings peace, including all in the process.[3] The families of Matara offer a vivid picture of *shalom,* of a village that knew its well-being was connected to the wellness of all its neighboring families despite tribal affiliation. Only when all families entered into equitable goodness did they experience *shalom.* And our Burundian friends will learn what a young Israel had to learn: Peaceableness requires continual maintenance.

During the extended time that the Israelites fled slavery

in Egypt, wandered in the wilderness for forty years, and finally crossed into the Promised Land, they learned about *shalom*-keeping the hard way. On the heels of their triumphant transition onto the land, the biblical narrative tells of a splintered *shalom*. Families were already fractured from within and warring without. Men were murdered, leaving women and children vulnerable in a patriarchal society. Land was stolen, expelling families from their ancestral homes and creating a poverty class. And wars broke out, introducing more loss of life, exile, and refugees. All this tumult left the families of Israel stressed and struggling. Creating instructions about the care of orphans, widows, and families at risk of falling into poverty became necessary to maintain the viability of the community at large. How these families embodied belonging would test the sustainability of *shalom*.

As the tribes of Israel showed signs of inner corrosion and began to buckle, God erected a scaffolding to protect both the needy and the neighborhood. Families would play a primary role in holding the nation together. Charged with offering hospitality to those widowed by violence or orphaned by disease or otherwise impoverished, families were the frontline for safeguarding their community. Taking in extended family members like nieces and nephews became a common custom, revealing that informal adoption was already a strategy employed for repairing neighborhoods.

Grafting vulnerable individuals, be they children or women, into existing family systems seemed to be the best way to protect them and the community at large.

God offered other corrective practices, structures of *shalom*, to secure stability for the entire region. One of those structures was gleaning rights, which provided access to food for those living on the underside of the economy. This was how Naomi and Ruth met their basic survival needs. Faithful practitioners of this structure like Boaz offered first fruits from their fields to God in thanksgiving and left their final fruits for neighbors like Naomi and Ruth, who, through no fault of their own, couldn't provide for themselves. So every plot of land, every field, provided for not just a single family but also the neighbor in need. This is where *tikkun olam* meets *shalom*, the recognition that repair work moves toward an expansive practice of equity. Each small gesture contributes to the common welfare.

Adoption is congruent with the *shalom* orientation we witness unfolding among the families of Israel. Families are core centers of belonging, possessing the capacity to enfold the most vulnerable ones. And each family can live in such a way as to provide for themselves and others who are at risk. One family might adopt an orphan and keep that child off the street or safe from a life of prostitution or banditry. Another family may manage their fields according to the Jubilee practice, so that families at risk can glean enough to eat and find their way back into the local economy. And all families are encouraged to practice hospitality with one another as well as the foreigners who cross through their land. Together, these families create the structures that help repair the community and ensure its viability.

Money cuts to the quick of what matters to us. Jesus says as much in Luke 12:34: "Where your heart is, there will your treasure be also." And money communicates volumes about belonging, influencing decisions about who is worthy of investment, who is deemed a drain on the system, and which community infrastructure projects get funded. Review any family, church, or city budget, and you'll know who does (and doesn't) matter.

Throughout Scripture, God consistently recognizes the connection between families and economies: they seem to rise and fall together. The prophets saw this too—how economic injustice was frequently the culprit tearing apart communities.[4] In Scripture, God repeatedly returns to the importance of an equitable economy for the health of each family and each community. In biblical narratives we can see that when the gap widens between the rich and the poor, families crack under the weight of the disparity. Clearly, God takes economics very seriously as a measure and a mechanism of community well-being.

Another special structure of *shalom* is Jubilee. At its most basic, it was an economic policy meant to redistribute land, debt, and labor toward greater equity, thus cultivating more viable communities.[5] And it's good to remember that when we talk about community, we're talking about a collection of families. Indeed, one of the first articulations of Jubilee puts families front and center. According to the Jubilee structure, the economy was reorganized every fifty years so that families could return to one another and their homestead.[6] This wise economic practice kept families together or created conditions for them to welcome (or adopt) others. Its focus put the health of families in full view.

When the Jubilee horn sounded across Israel in the fiftieth year, all debts were forgiven, land was returned to original owners, and slaves were set free. Whatever was confiscated in the last generation's economic downturn could be reclaimed. And, to be clear, this meant the forgiveness of family debt and the return of family land so that families could experience repair and a second chance. According to Jubilee economics, no one should live in perpetual poverty or forever be locked out of the life of the neighborhood. Families shouldn't be trapped in cycles of poverty generation after generation. As hard as it was (and it was), some families gave back so other families could start again. Jubilee was one mechanism meant to ensure that everyone could live well in the neighborhood.

To the modern ear, Jubilee sounds preposterous, too utopian to be true. But evidence exists that Jubilee practices did occur on a small scale. And more to the point, Jubilee is aspirational. It provides a way to see how a well-ordered economy could move entire communities toward wholeness.

For the prophet Isaiah, the economy was an integral strand in rebuilding Jerusalem after its destruction. Exploitive practices that allowed the rich to pry land from their neighbors, saddle them with debt, and enslave them would not make Jerusalem great again. The economy had to be calibrated to work for every family, so repair work had to include the economy; it had to address the lives and the livelihood of every family in the city. Larger economic systems impinged on families then just as they do now. Consider foreclosures on family homes due to economic speculation, or low wages that demand full-time work from parents but still result in life below the poverty line, and you see how impersonal structures weigh on individual families. These are the very kinds of economics that can push families apart. All the more reason to be mindful of them as we consider how we can be involved in repair work.

What would it look like to be involved in economic repair for the sake of our family and communities? Again, from the mountains of Matara in Burundi we find an example. Even though some tribal tensions had eased, our Batwa friends were still in the thick of their campaign to make a lasting peace with their neighbors. So they bought pigs, enough for each family in their village. Together they decided that the first litter of pigs would stay in the village, but the second litter would be gifted to their neighbors. Each family agreed to this, meaning that soon thirty litters would be given away to contribute to the household incomes of the entire community. No one mandated this gift; no one followed a biblical imperative on purpose. But the Batwa families lived into the Jubilee spirit with their concrete generosity, care for neighbors, and desire to see all the villages thrive.

The pigs represented a source of income for each family. The first litter increased the income of a Batwa family, and the second litter increased the income of a family in a neighboring village. This meant that more families experienced increase and could provide for their children. A better economic capacity in turn meant that each family had a better chance of buying what they needed at market, getting medicine for a sick child, and paying school fees for their sons and daughters. It meant some families would have enough income to adopt their brother's children in the wake of his death. This strengthening of families throughout the Matara region made for a more viable and vibrant community for all their children. This is what Isaiah imagined could happen—lives and livelihoods strengthened for the good of the community.

These families, looking out for both themselves and their neighbors, are less likely to be anyone's victim. Who would try to entice them to relinquish their children in exchange for money? These families are doing well enough that they aren't vulnerable to such ploys and would easily rebuff them. The message is clear: Keeping these families strong and economically viable keeps them intact. As we explore the metaphor and reality of adoption, we must care about preventing any injustice this side of heaven that creates the need for the repair work of adoption.

Adoption enacts *shalom* for all of us, families as well as communities. As a family receives a child, they demonstrate the radical hospitality of God's *shalom*. Each family member is ripe for transformation as they experience a family bond stronger than bloodlines or ethnic division. Communities seeded with such families witness the capacity to enfold the disenfranchised ones as kin. And a community comprised of such families provides a place where fewer are left on the margins and more are welcomed around the dinner table. Taken together, such communities begin to evidence the stability of a *shalom*-shaped society.

Adoption isn't only for or about orphans. Adoption is about enacting *shalom* for all of us.

For some families and even churches engaged in questions surrounding adoption, their starting question is "Should we adopt?" or "Am I called to adopt?" or "How do we support adoption?" But I believe these questions aren't scripturally informed. In the biblical narratives, from Moses to Ruth, the question we see asked is different: How might we best contribute to God's *shalom* initiative? We have in common the biblical imperative to increase the well-being not only of our families, but of our communities. The challenge facing each of us is to discover how we are invited to join God's comprehensive campaign of *shalom*. Adoption is one way to strengthen the neighborhood—but there are also other paths and callings in a much larger consideration and context.

We are called to care for the well-being of everyone in our community, but especially the vulnerable ones. Strengthening the neighborhood will mean taking many and varied approaches to enfold a variety of vulnerable people— not only orphans but families at risk, refugees, immigrants, the homeless, and those on the fringe in our neighborhood.

Looking deeply into a campaign of *shalom*, we also see the needs of single-parent families, parents struggling to earn enough to provide for the basics while making enough time to be present to their children and still finding room to rest. My friend Sarah, who's single with no children of her own, offers childcare for a single parent on a regular basis. The mother, a flight attendant, sometimes needs to work overnight shifts, but she can trust her children to the care of this reliable friend. And as I watch Sarah collaborate with this mother, juggling schedules and stretching herself to be of help, I see that she contributes to the *shalom* of a household, the stability of this family. If more people saw the larger vision of *shalom* for our communities, they would shore up the worn places for single-parent families by extending not only friendship but also practical assistance like childcare and financial help. These families so supported and strengthened would make entire communities stronger.

Practicing *shalom* means that we're reaching out to help families at risk, those below the poverty line or on the downside of the economy. They may be refugee families living in the slums of our inner cities without adequate infrastructure or access to needed services. They may be families living in depressed neighborhoods with poor-performing public schools. In the spirit of *shalom*, might we take on the challenge to advocate for these families? What might it look like to consider standing up for better wages, better working conditions, better schools, and more support services as a means of expressing our commitment to family values, knowing how profoundly economic policy is connected to family health and viability? Surely supporting families on the brink is part of strengthening the community.

Often families living in poverty lack not only money but

also education, healthcare, and food security. Under unjust global systems, these at-risk ones are pressured into making heart-rending choices about how to manage their family. The parents often fall victim to those who would exploit their poverty—people who would give them money in exchange for an infant (which the at-risk accept under duress) or fool them into signing documents that sever their rights to their children. Without doubt this is the kind of injustice God hates.

As parents of children once orphaned by disease and poverty, Claude and I are familiar with the kind of injustice that creates vulnerable children. Our commitment to *shalom* for communities led us to engage in community development work in Burundi so that these families would never be tempted or tricked into relinquishing their children. Enriching these communities with agriculture, clean water, good schools, health clinics, access to loans, and better housing has become our way of incarnating the Jubilee for the sake of these families. For us, working to prevent the conditions that necessitate adoption is also *shalom*-shaped work. When a family can stay intact, then *shalom* is served, justice is winning the day.

Others share this call for pre-emptive justice. My friends Troy and Tara Livesay operate a maternity clinic and midwifery program in Haiti so that mothers can keep their children and not be forced to relinquish them unnecessarily.

They also offer parenting classes and maintain a literacy program for the mothers so they can provide stability for their families in years to come. Another friend of mine is taking his place as a watchdog regarding adoption ethics. Seth partners with colleagues in Ethiopia to support ethical adoptions and, as a lawyer, extends ad-hoc advice to American couples who want to steer clear of exploiting poor families unintentionally. Doing this kind of work or funding it are other ways to strengthen vulnerable families. Adoption is a holy means of establishing belonging after relinquishment; but holy is the work that strengthens families before relinquishment is necessary.

When we safeguard the rights of these families, advocate for better policies on their behalf, and partner with them to find solutions, we're participating in the work of *shalom*. This kind of engagement bears witness to our family values, the ones rooted in the biblical text.

Adoption is *how* we tend to orphans, but it is sourced in *shalom*. Indeed, adoption can be a tangible sign of *shalom* in our imperfect world. I know this firsthand because adoption grafted me into a family tree. Adoption kept me out of the foster care system. And adoption was the invitation my husband and I received when we met our two children: to enfold them into a family and community so they wouldn't end up on the dusty streets of Bujumbura.

Adoption is a modern structure of *shalom* able to repair

some of the torn places in our world. And it's one of many ways to move toward *tikkun olam* and the New City.

Adoption stretches beyond parents and children. It's how we embody family, welcoming others into relationships that give them a place to be accepted and safe. It's how we cultivate belonging in our neighborhoods, churches, and communities. Each adoptive gesture contributes to the repair of those torn places in our world.

The current political challenges in Burundi force families to make hard choices about their safety. Our long-time friend Emery had to send his family out of the country to ensure that they would not be harassed or harmed. Without his wife and kids, he turned to Claude and asked if he could live with us in the interim. We had a spare room and, more important, a willingness to include him in our family. Now he comes and goes as easily as any of us do through the hallways of the house. He watches soccer matches with my son and knows what kind of muffins my kids like to snack on. He brings me cases of sparkling water and runs household errands without complaint. He looks out for us, and we keep up with him. Until his family can be reunited, we're glad to be together. We are family; we've adopted each other.

Jason and Heather are the godparents of our children. Certain legal implications might come into effect should the worst happen to Claude and me, but for now they're under little obligation. Yet they've adopted my kids already. They never miss celebrating a birthday or a holiday. Uncle Jason tried to teach Justin to ride a bike. Aunt Heather has taught my son and daughter how to make her signature chocolate cake. The two of them regularly pack up their Volvo and drive from California to spend time with us when we're stateside, long visits where we can get into the mess of life together, as siblings do. They're not waiting to step in and care for our children. They're already assuming their roles as adoptive ones, already enfolding us into their lives in sacrificial and life-giving ways.

Adoption is a way of life, a way of making belonging visible. Maybe adoption best describes how Tahany and I jumped into each other's lives—how I cared for her boys, and how she invited me into the delivery room for the birth of her third son, and how we'll be together in her home in Palestine soon. Maybe adoption makes the most sense of how Janelle has mothered me through some hard seasons, seeing me as her own. Maybe adoption helps us understand how two different communities, one from suburban Texas and one from rural Burundi, can be friends who celebrate births and new churches together. I'll never forget when our Batwa friends prayed fervently over months and miles for a friend in Texas with a dire cancer diagnosis—and how they danced together when she was strong enough to travel to Matara and spend the night in their village. All different kinds of adoption can bind us together.

We miss the potency of adoption when we limit it to a legal mechanism to make children part of a family. Adoption is so much more—a deep and multifaceted way we incarnate *shalom* in our community. We enfold one another into our family in tangible ways by welcoming, reciprocating care, and redeeming the broken places as we care for one another. And the beauty is that we can cross all manner of boundaries to be family. We're not limited by bloodlines or ethnicity or even nationality. Anyone can be our family if we let them.

In the days of the biblical prophets, after the demise of their beloved city, the Jews returned to their land to rebuild Jerusalem and reimagine their future after over a generation in exile. Many different voices joined in the conversation about the urban reconstruction project. Nehemiah and Ezra had their plans for revitalization, which included repair of the outer wall of the city, teaching Torah so Jews could worship once again, and reclaiming ethnic purity by ceasing all intermarriage with foreigners.[7] Only one prophet—Isaiah—stood apart. His vision for the New City was different—a vision of inclusion, justice, and neighborliness.

Belonging mends our world. For Isaiah, membership in the New City was to be inclusive—even eunuchs and foreigners could join in if they kept Sabbath and covenant. At the time, this was like saying that traitors and enemies were welcome—but the prophet dreamed a daring, holy dream about the kind of city God wanted. In this city, the prophet affirmed, everyone would be allowed to worship, and the new temple would be a house of prayer for all people. And Isaiah further declared that Jubilee economics would ensure equity for all. The dream was to have an economy calibrated to support every family so that all could thrive in the city God designed.

In this New City, everyone could imagine a full life. Wherever you came from, whatever your economic class, as long as you honored God and were a good neighbor, you could call this place your home. And the prophet went even further—you will all be kin, he said, one seamless family. It takes your breath away, the expansiveness of this vision, or it scares you a bit. But the writing of Isaiah is one sweeping poem that is part of our canon, part of the biblical conversation about how to make Israel great again. Some thought greatness could be achieved by purity and exclusionary policies, but Isaiah wagered on inclusivity and welcome.

Adoption is a sacrament of resistance, pushing back against xenophobia, estrangement, loneliness, and the invisibility of the vulnerable. Every instance of belonging says no to orphanhood, no to fending for yourself, no to scarce resources, no to relinquishment having the last word. And every time we adopt, in the largest sense of the word, we resist exclusion and engage in the repair work that restores neighborhoods and rebuilds cities. Adoption builds the New City. Belonging mends the world.

CHAPTER SEVEN

Return

Part of adoption, in the aftermath of relinquishment and even the afterglow of redemption, is the pull toward repatriation. Adopted ones find ourselves longing to know more—to view medical records, to learn our physical history, to hear stories. Sometimes we search for birth parents or want to visit our homeland. It's only natural.

This longing for our first home, our first mother, is not a lack of gratitude for the adoptive sacrament or disrespect for those who've adopted us. Nor is it a deficiency in an adoptive home that creates this hunger for other parents, other places, other times before relinquishment. Late in my own adoptive life, I discovered that longing for first things wasn't about a lack, but about another kind of fullness entirely. What I longed for was a wholeness that included an understanding of my roots and the soil indigenous to my feet.

At some point our curiosities emerge, along with a desire

to know what lurks in the corners of our own story, that unread chapter that might provide pivotal information about our origins. We want to connect to our own creation narrative. We come around early or late, but all of us have curiosities about home.

While it may seem to be a counterintuitive move, seeking repatriation opens us to futures that we can only realize through this process.

The Dome of the Rock holds particular sway over my imagination. It shimmers like a crown jewel in gold and sapphire hues on the Jerusalem skyline. This city, at once ancient and modern, boasts of a hallowed past and a holy future. It is sacred ground for many of the world's devout. It's also hotly contested territory.

Under the golden dome, within the mosaic walls, rests the foundation stone, the original rock plateau where the first worshipers, the Jebusites, christened the land with prayer and dance. King David conquered and consecrated the location. His son, Solomon, built the first temple here, and the Ark of the Covenant and the Shekinah (glory) of God resided here. At one point it was destroyed, lying in cold ruins until the second temple reconstruction began. Once completed, the second temple was more glorious than the first. While this temple was also destroyed, the plateau remains, the epicenter for all that is holy to Jews and, by extension, Christians.

Legend has it that Abraham's binding of Isaac (or Ishmael, as our Muslim friends believe) happened here. The sacrifice and rescue on this spot makes this a significant site for all the Abrahamic faith traditions. Muslims believe that when Muhammad took his Night Journey from Mecca to "the farthest mosque," he arrived at this rock. And from this rock he ascended to heaven to consult with Allah. Some say this is where he met with Abraham, Moses, and Jesus.

It's not easy to share our altars across religious lines, and here we particularly find ourselves between this rock and a hard place. The Dome of the Rock, perched on the Temple Mount, is the vortex of our current animosity, as Muslims, Jews, and Christians contend for control of Jerusalem and superiority over peace. We struggle—often in vain—to honor one another, to acknowledge what is held between us. We routinely deface the image of God in one another, ignoring the common instruction we share imploring us to honor the humanity in each other. Sometimes even our faiths can't save us from our anti-*shalom* tendencies.

My imagination sputters and sparks with the thought of this shared point of origin. According to some Jewish traditions, this is the place where genesis spun outward from God's own hand. Across the generations we've been lured upward to this rock by the Psalmist's songs of ascent. A magnetism draws pilgrims from the Jewish diaspora, attracts the Christian devout, and calls to Muslims. Jerusalem is a sacred space jointly cherished, exclusive to none. And while a current locus of strife and struggle, it was once the wellspring of faith, and will one day be the site of a great convergence. The prophets say that God's temple will, at last, be a house of prayer for all nations, the place of our hoped-for repatriation.

In my mid-thirties I began to experience a shift in my relationship with my mother. My changing view on politics and polity wedged us apart. I became a disappointment to her. This widening rift between us cracked me open in more ways than I realized.

Around this time I craved a return to my Catholic roots. (My parents had left the Catholic Church when I was in middle school, and I had migrated with them.) I desired a more contemplative space. I hungered for weekly bread and wine and the passing of the peace one to another. I wanted to hear Psalms read aloud and pray the Lord's Prayer in unison with others. What drew me back were my memories of flickering flames flaring out of cobalt-blue votives, and rosary beads slipping through my hands, and the sound of shoes shuffling down the aisle as believers queued to receive the sacrament. I remembered the luminous icon of Mary holding her holy son. I wanted to stand before her again.

When I walked into Saint Clare of Assisi's on Ash Wednesday, I dipped my fingers into the basin of cool water in the sanctuary. I made the sign of the cross, blessing dripping from my fingers. I centered myself in the space, breathing it all in. The smell of vigil candles mingled with incense clung to the air, the aroma of invitation. Mother Mary, glowing gold, held court over the rows of candles, holding up her half of the sapphire-painted sky. And with arms outstretched, Christ hung over the altar, welcoming me home.

I found comfort in the nave of the cathedral. My shoulders dropped; my breath slowed. So I kept returning, week after week. I heard my mother tongue spoken. I stood, knelt, processed. And I recovered something indigenous to me.

It would be another season before I found the language for what I felt in the return to my Catholic roots. Speaking to a gathering of the faithful in Albuquerque, Phyllis Tickle was explaining the cyclical movements of church history when she limned the image of *Mother Church*. Sitting in that hotel ballroom, I knew she had just described my relationship with the Catholic Church: *mother.* She'd been wooing and welcoming me home.

This mother invited me to come and sit, to eat, pray, and be blessed in her company. She wasn't perfect—no mother is—but she was kind when I needed kindness and offered me a connection I'd lost. I grew increasingly grateful for the embrace of my Mother Church at a time when my own mother felt more distant.

Now I understand how my Mother Church holds my cherished firsts: my first confession, my first communion, and even my first experience of catechism. Amid the height of the charismatic renewal movement, I learned to sing praise songs and shake my shellacked tambourine in the fellowship hall of Saint Nicholas Church. Under the canopy of my Mother Church, I spoke in tongues and was baptized in the Spirit. My most formative sacrament, adoption, happened by her hand through the Holy Family Adoption Agency. And it was her band of faithful women who surrounded me, dipping my bald, pink head into baptismal waters and identifying me as hers.

She is the birth mother I never knew I needed until I was older. Since returning to her, I stand more deeply rooted in my own story. My own identity seems less shrouded, though mystery will always remain.

Maybe Jesus walked the distance from the backwater of Nazareth to the Jordan River unaware of what he needed, too. He shuffled down the brown banks to join his cousin, John the Baptist, already waist-high in the water. Away from the temple, with its straitjacketed religious strictures and exclusionary tendencies, Jesus stripped off his clothes. He waded into the river, hungry for a cleansing.

He succumbed to the Baptist and the waters, then rose into a new identity. The Gospels agree that once he came out from the water, the Spirit descended like a dove. Then a Voice from heaven said, "This is my beloved Son, with whom I am well pleased."[1] These are the exact words Jewish fathers say over a newborn son, confirming paternity and declaring sonship in unambiguous terms.[2]

Was the voice audible to the crowd, or was this moment between a father and a son too intimate for an audience? Standing drenched in the Jordan River, Jesus learned about his First Father and his heavenly origin. He understood his identity more fully—as both divine and human, of kin with the Creator and yet a creature, too. God revealed the true nature of their relationship: Spirit of my Spirit, not One but Three, an unimaginable incarnation.

Imagine Jesus awash in Spirit and knee-deep in revelation. He isn't an oddity, an unexplained theological prodigy able to astonish the temple scholars—he is his Father's Son. The origin of his exceptionalism finally explained, he is both the Father's only Son and Joseph's firstborn. His identity gives him confidence and initiates a fullness of self-knowledge that will propel him into public life.

What was visible to those on the banks of the river that day? Jesus baptized, rising from the waters somehow transformed, more deeply himself. What stood apparent was a mysterious dynamic at work, best described by all the Gospel witnesses as a dove descending from heaven. It is the only way you can picture the metamorphosis, they say. Something indescribable happened—like a bird hovering over creation or a dove returning to the ark with a branch of hope.

This is the scene so many adopted ones long for: the discovery of a birth parent. We want that dark corner illuminated. We imagine our own transformation at the revelation of our true origin. What goodness might be unlocked, what possibility unleashed? No one experiences adoption without wrestling, a lot or a little, with these original curiosities. So it's a kind of catharsis to see Jesus, the Adopted One, receive the revelation and recognition that many in the company of the adopted crave.

But not all adopted ones get a repatriation of heart. Many corners of our story may remain a mystery—medical records are a blank, adoption documents remain sealed, and parts of our story die without our ever knowing. For many this is an incessant pang, persistent anguish over a kind of return they're denied.

But return is not unique to adopted ones. All of us reach back to the homes where we grew up and the streets of our childhood, return to high school reunions and alma maters in search of reconnection or reaffirmation. What is good in us? What can be reclaimed and repurposed? What might the search for our ancestry reveal—and why does it matter that our great-great-grandmother was the first to graduate from college in her small town, that our father's lineage boasts many artists or business owners or inventors, that we share genes with an original abolitionist? Maybe we're coming to see the deep pull of those biblical genealogies we once so glibly skipped over. Because origins matter.

My own children won't know their birth parents, but they do have the gift of their Burundian culture. Alongside the undeniable sadness that Emma won't ever get to see her birth mother or know her name lives the graceful sway of her adolescent hips as she learns the traditional Burundian dance. Justin won't know why, exactly, he was relinquished, but he speaks his mother tongue of Kirundi, loves soccer, French rap, and sambusas. Both of them possess a Burundian heartbeat pounded out by burnished drummers under the molten sun, and though it's not consolation enough for all that relinquishment entails, it is still an inheritance they can treasure.

International adoptions (or transracial ones) often lift children out of their cultural context and graft them into a new family and culture simultaneously. It's why I've always told my children they are Burundian-American, to make sure they know that both cultures inform who they are and who they will become on this earth. They've been told from their toddling years that their adventure is to discover what it means to be both a Burundian and an American. In what unique ways will they embrace and embody these cultures?

Because of the development work that Claude and I do, our children have the unique opportunity to live between Burundi and America. They get to know the gentle slope of the foothills of Bujumbura dropping into the depths of Lake Tanganyika, to grow up with a horizon filled with the massive Congolese mountains across waters populated with hippos. The languages of their homeland are like a mixtape on repeat—Kirundi and French melodies punctuated by Swahili phrases and Arabic words like a strike of the hi-hat cymbal. Their traditions aren't a mystery to them, even if their genealogy remains unknowable.

Criss-crossing the small, dusty capital city, we drive with the windows rolled down. The smells offer another signature—roasting meats on open clay *imbaburas,* sun-dried linens, sweet mandarins, and sweat. We move out past the slums, cutting across the countryside with too many shades of green to count. Our two kids are buckled in the back-seat, staring out the windows, inhaling their birthright. It is theirs—to be absorbed by or bored by. Justin's soul mingles with this soil, an irrevocable force that dwarfs the power of passports, birth certificates, and adoption decrees. This landscape belongs to Emma, too. Each drive is a small turn-ing toward home, their young selves returning to Eden. And I know that it is very good.

My husband, his large family, and his endless stream of cousins mediate Burundian culture for our children. Most adopted children and their families don't have such a direct link and bevy of relatives at the ready to convey culture, and too often families resort to an unintended cultural kitsch. As a hat-tip to the country of origin of our adopted children, we go to an Ethiopian restaurant or get Chinese take-out or buy Starbucks' Guatemala Antigua coffee—as if that's enough. Our penchant to insert foreign costumes, holidays, and flags into their lives runs the risk of creating isolation instead of integration. Appropriating culture in sentimental ways singles out our children, making their cultural artifacts an uneasy reminder of connections they don't have and traditions we don't understand. Thoughtful and continual discernment move us from simple fascination to engaged fidelity with adopted cultures for the sake of our children.

But how powerful it is when our children can return, in whatever way available to them, and reclaim their roots. Each will be able to return to us with riches to share with the entire family. My own children (and husband) have given me a connection to Burundi, the beauty and complexity of it adding to the texture of our family life. For me, it has also broken the hold of American exceptionalism and tendencies toward xenophobia embedded since my childhood. Solidarity with this small African nation has altered my perspective on security, necessity, privilege, and poverty and enriched my children's lives immeasurably. Returning to one's roots can be a communal, transformational blessing.

When I consider the blessing of knowing where you've come from and finding a means for return, I think of the history stolen from my African-American brothers and sisters. Violently pulled from their roots, the soil that gave them life and identity, they continue to suffer that savage injustice.

In 2016 the mini-series *Roots* was remade and telecast for a new generation. It's an adaptation of Alex Haley's novel about an African man sold into slavery and the struggle of his descendants toward emancipation. In response to the first night's episode, focusing on the kidnapping and transport of her descendants to the South, Lisa Sharon Harper wrote a visceral poem:

> *Primal scream rises from beneath layers of armor—saggy pants, hoodies, bow ties, weaves. "Don't forget me," it cries to Africa!*
>
> *The scream rumbles through heart and limbs, reaching out. Rage rises. Songs pierce armor: "Don't forget us," Africa whispers back.*[3]

Even after generations apart, the two long for one another. The bond between land and people is unbreakable, and the injustice of a long-ago separation still levies a toll. This doesn't diminish America as home but, as Lisa Sharon Harper testifies, roots remain and cry out for return. They also cry out for justice.

Now waves of Nigerians are returning to their homeland. Children of migrants who moved to the West for work at one time, these grown children now want to know Nigeria with their own senses. It's not uncommon for refugee families resettled in the West to imagine repatriation, to hold out hope that their homeland's brokenness will be healed and their connection can remain, even if they cannot live there again.

Other places call us home. And I don't know how we mete out justice for those taken or forced out. I only know that the land cries out, that souls hunger for home, and that justice demands our power of prophetic imagination to open the gates for return.

Jubilee is the twin sister of justice. In Leviticus 25, Moses wrote, "*It shall be a year of jubilee for you: you shall return, every one of you, to your property, and every one of you to your family.*" The goodness of a re-calibrated economy is predicated on tangible return—repatriation to your land and to your family.

Imagine what the return of Jubilee would look like. The

horn blows on the morning of the fiftieth year. The initial scramble comes from the landowners, the deed holders, the ones who will see their gains diminished before sunset. It's a hard day for them, this obedience to God which curbs their acquisitiveness. But deeds are returned to original holders, slaves are set free, and IOU's are voided once and for all. And the migration home begins. . . .

A man makes his way home, his eyes soaking in the land that was his father's and his grandfather's before him. He squints to see the house in the distance, the one he built with his own hands. As he approaches, she comes into view. Her scars show the years have been hard on her, too. By the time he's at her side, his daughters grab his legs, orphaned no more. It would be the next evening before the table was complete—when their son, now marrying age, returned to take his position alongside his father. The family offers thanksgiving to the God who still liberates, who always brings them home. Tomorrow they will begin again—taking the small compensation they were given to buy some seed and plant once more. But for now they can rest because they are where they belong.

True liberation, among other things, meant a return to ancestral land and to the fullness of family—the complete embodiment of homecoming, every family member returning to the homestead. Such widespread reunion would have implications for the entire neighborhood as family upon family re-entered the economy to rebuild a viable and vibrant community.

With Jubilee on his lips, the prophet Isaiah declared the goodness of return for a displaced people. After several generations of exile in Babylon, the Jews were able to return to Jerusalem, return to the foundation stone and rebuild the temple. God knew that returning matters. Return was perfumed with justice, the scent of *shalom* thick around the shoulders of our ancestors as they walked home. Once they arrived in the ruined city, they gathered up their courage and began the repair work—starting, I hope, with the economy predicated on Jubilee.

In 1948 the world was still recovering from World War II, trying to repair the violent tearing in the fabric of humanity caused by the Holocaust. But how do you address the loss of eleven million people? The United Nations agreed that one way might be making a way for Jews to return, somehow, to a place of safety. And so in 1948 the State of Israel was born.

Return for one traumatized people created a new legacy of trauma for another. Those living in Palestine were pushed out, with pots of food still simmering on stoves, some say.[4] The Nakba—"The Catastrophe," as it's called—displaced more than 700,000 Arab Palestinians. Forced off their land and out of their homes, today these families are scattered throughout the West Bank and Gaza, in refugee camps in Lebanon, Jordan, and Syria. In 1948 the United Nations General Assembly passed Resolution #194, recognizing the right of return for refugees. In 1974 another resolution declared the right of return an inalienable right. But none of this was legally binding, the now entrenched State of Israel countered. And so the refugees and their descendants, now numbering over four million worldwide, live apart from their homeland.

I remember the Saturday morning I sat with Tahany and Khalid under the generous shade trees in the park near my home, watching our kids on the playground. Khalid told me of his own family, his father, forced out of his home. He pitched a tent on the outskirts of the town, certain this eviction was temporary. But help never came. Eventually there was no choice but to flee to the West Bank to live, mourn, and wait for return. Khalid's entire family still waits. Even as they live between Ramallah and Arizona, they still dream of going home to their father's house. I know about the Nakba, but his family lives the tragedy every day.

A certain kind of pain strikes when return is forbidden. I think of the old proverb about hope deferred making the heart sick.[5] How riddled with sickness are the Occupied Territories, the bulging refugee camps! Listen to their poets and know that the ache remains, as does the dream of repatriation.

I hope with my friends that one day there will be a return. My imagination is funded by the God who returns land to out-of-luck families, returns exiles to Jerusalem, and returns a once-dead Lazarus back to life and back into the arms of his sisters. I think of Naomi repatriating and finding redemption, Moses returning to Egypt to enact emancipation. I consider the deep yearning of the cosmos to return to the original *shalom* of Eden.

The day we left the Rainbow Center, a home for abandoned babies where our children lived the first chapter of their lives, was bittersweet. With our two toddlers we drove to the airport in a caravan, the nannies piled in the van behind us. It is very Burundian to want to offer a gracious send-off, and these women went as far as airport security would allow them. As they kissed Justin and Emma good-bye, I saw how well loved our children already were, and how they'd be missed by these women.

Five years later, we returned to the Rainbow Center. In honor of their Adoption Day, Claude and I took Justin and Emma back to visit the small house where they became siblings, cribs side by side in the back room. This was a time for them to see with older eyes and sharper memories the place where they had spent their earliest days. It was also a time to say thank you to the nannies who cared for them all those months.

We arrived unannounced. One woman peeked out the swinging red doors and then came out to greet us. As soon as she saw Justin pop out of the car, she recognized him—those dimples are a dead give-away! She shouted something in Kirundi and then, like a colony of ants, the nannies swarmed out of the small house. They ran to the car and shrieked with joy when they saw him, eight years old and handsome, "just like I remembered," one said. But when Emma got out of the other side of the car and joined her brother, a hush came over the women. They looked at her, at one another, and asked Claude if this could really be *her.*

When these women last saw Emma, she was still under a hospice order. She was smiling by then, but still swollen. But now she stood beside her brother, healthy and lovelier than they might ever have imagined. Once it sunk in, the women couldn't stop touching her, hugging her as if she was the resurrected Christ before their Easter eyes. When she went to join the other kids on the playground, the nannies followed and watched her, cooing and laughing in amazement. It was clear that both Emma and Justin still belonged to them.

Stepping back into that chapter of their story allowed Justin and Emma to see how and where they were loved before we adopted them. Their return to the Rainbow Center also allowed them to say thank you to every nanny, to give tangible affirmation to these faithful women. Together we remembered the ways in which we continued to belong to

each other, our stories forever linked, our gratitude boundless for a return that was a blessing for us all.

We all carry an urge to return. Instinctively we know there
are riches to be mined, gems of goodness to bring back to
the communities we belong to. The treasure may reside in
our homeland's culture or landscape. It may be found in a
reunion with a birth parent or distant relative. Maybe hidden
in the embrace of our Mother Church is the acceptance we
long to know. We may need to return to the time before the
hurt happened to find the resources that will help us imagine
forgiveness.

Mysterious as it may sound, repatriation belongs in the
rubric of belonging. We return for identity's sake, for the
sake of wholeness and redemption. We return to right historic and enduring wrongs with confession, contrition, and
repentance. We try to do the unimaginable and join the Lord
of all creation in the reconciling of all things.

But a full revelation or reunion isn't always possible. Our
birth parents have died; our records are lost. Check points
bar us from returning; walls separate us from people and
places that hold our heart. And how do we right a wrong
from generations ago? We see in part; maybe we only return
in part, too.

But sometimes hope sprouts, and our splintered neighborhoods and broken-down cities begin to rise from the ashes of injustice. Then the indescribable happens. As relationships experience the balm of forgiveness and we are healed—so are the nations. The mysterious dynamic of repatriation is at work once again as small returns occur. Like that day in the Jordan River when, for lack of a better description, a dove descended, a day comes when we see a new city descend. How else can we describe the unimaginable transformation?

The Apostle John, late in his life and deep in exile on the island of Patmos, dreamed such a thing might happen. He saw a new heaven and a new earth emerge. He saw the old heaven and the old earth pass away—become less real somehow. "I saw the holy city, the new Jerusalem, descending from heaven," he said in language both cryptic and true. In this city, he said, there will be no more tears or death or mourning, no more crying or pain. And no one will be left out because "its gates will never be closed."[6] We will always be free to return to the restored and yet new city.

Isaiah's dream returns us to the foundation stone on the Temple Mount, God bringing us back to the holy mountain. "For my house will be called a house of prayer for all peoples," God declares.[7] There will be a great and generous gathering of the diaspora, the prophet says. No one will be left out of the return parade God designs. Imagine displaced peoples and refugees returning. Imagine our African-

American brothers and sisters finally returning, adoptees and immigrants and the displaced parts of us, all repatriates in God's temple.

This is the very foundation for the world God envisions, all the adopted ones home at last and worshiping together on the holy mountain. It is an ascent that echoes the descent of the New City. Two visions of the same truth: With God there is always the hope of return. Roads are prepared and gates remain open.

CHAPTER EIGHT

Relatives

I t's inevitable. Every adopted child gets asked, "But who's your *real* mother?" or "Do you know your *real* family?" The assumption is that our adoptive family isn't entirely real. We are a muddled copy of the original, a second-generation recording a bit deficient in quality.

Is a family that is shaped by adoption unnatural? Those who ask might have little connection to an adoptive family and really not know the answer. Or perhaps they can't imagine that belonging creates a bond as strong as biology. While the questions threaten our sense of family and our very identity, those same questions become an opportunity to break open our sacrament, sharing what we've learned round our family table.

If adopted families are an anomaly, we skew supranatural. We have learned how to belong to one another beyond the boundaries. Our formation allows us to cultivate belonging with anyone unlike us because we know that it's always possible to graft someone into our family tree. Point us to the arid places, and we will break the ground and plow it toward connection and kinship. It is our superpower.

But it seems our belonging is often under investigation. Ask any immigrant, and they will tell you that people want to know where they're from and just as quickly ask when they plan to go back. We are suspicious of difference, and it only takes a slight accent or missed cultural cue for insiders to determine who's an outsider and call their allegiance into question. People doubt that connection can coincide with great difference—biological, cultural, or otherwise. But the truth is, we can just as easily be wary of someone from another church, another faith tradition, or an opposing political party. We behave like we're different species instead of fellow siblings in God's wide family.

God's family stretches beyond our smaller notions of biological or ethnic connection. The other is always much closer to being our kin than we imagine. It's the continual work of the prophets and the Spirit to open our eyes to this simple yet astounding truth: Anyone can be our family if we let them. With eyes opened, we realize we are a family so wide with welcome that enemy love is inevitable. Eventually, contrary to the current world order, even our enemy can become our flesh.

I first met Richard Twiss in the Amsterdam airport. His long hair, dark and lustrous as onyx, was gathered into a ponytail that ran the length of his spine. He towered over us mortals at the gate, especially my family of short stature. But his intimidating height was instantly tempered by his wide smile. We were Rwanda-bound for the second annual Amahoro Gathering, and got a head-start with introductions as we waited to board the long flight between continents.

A Sicangu Lakota, Richard often spoke of the injustices done to his people since the inception of our country, wrongs that endure today. He exhorted us to recognize our shared history and move toward repentance so that we could walk in reconciled relationship together in this land. He was as blunt as he was tall. If it wasn't for his wicked sense of humor, I don't know how we'd have survived his brutal honesty in naming the wrongs inflicted on the Native American communities.

This made his characteristic greeting all the more stunning. He would stand before us and in his Lakota mother tongue address us, the historic oppressors of his people, as *"Mitakuye Oyasin."* Without any sense of irony, he recognized us as "all my relatives." He explained the nature of our interconnection, as understood by his ancestors, to one another and the land we jointly inhabit. As far as Richard was concerned, we were all relatives, despite the unresolved issues among us. And because we were family, he refused to be coy about the fractured state of our relationship and what must be explored so we can move toward *shalom* as siblings in God's family.

When I learned that Richard died in February of 2013, it hit me hard. I felt as if my own brother had left me too soon. It's a testament to how fully he embodied the deep relatedness and fidelity of *Mitakuye Oyasin* that I feel his absence still. His unrelenting insistence that we were family stays with me.

The quickest way to undermine the sacrament of belonging is to say that it's not natural. We often hear this in ways both subtle and blatant. I hear it when I'm asked about my *real* mother, or when I'm asked if my children are *at least* biological siblings. We hear it when people agree that raising adopted children, while laudable, is harder because "they aren't your natural children." Or when people talk about adopting as a distant second (or third) option for growing their family, a strategy they'll employ only after they've exhausted all other options (including their spent savings and fatigued bodies due to the economic and physical rigors of multiple IVF procedures). When adoption is treated this way—as secondhand, second-best, or unnatural—it hurts. Even describing adoption as benevolent but less than biological child-bearing sullies the sacred way God shaped my family and many others.

People mean well. And, after all, I'm not that fragile. But the message of "good but not natural" doesn't ring true to those who drink from the chalice of the adoptive sacrament daily, imbibing the family grace. No. In a God-ordained family, it doesn't feel unnatural. Most of us are naked and unashamed in our homes, crawling under the covers with our mothers and wrestling barefoot with our siblings and laughing with our superhero fathers. We're at home where we belong, naturally.

In our home, ringed by adoption goodness, I am many things: tantrum-wrangler, nightmare-whisperer, Band-Aid dispenser. I am oatmeal-maker, bedside intercessor, conversation partner, affirmation muse, and a conveyer belt of hugs, kisses, and cheeky squeezes. I am not, however, unnatural. I'm not a secondhand mother, a lesser choice for these babes of mine. Nor was my own mother anything less than a natural fit for me. When God is in the family way, it might look mysterious, but never unnatural.

The supra-natural truth that adoption demonstrates is that any child could be mine if I welcome them. Any kid on the dusty streets of Bujumbura, any girl walking into the international school in her crisp uniform, or any lone boy in a suburban neighborhood could be mine. Likewise, any woman could be my mother, any one my sister—it doesn't matter if she's Palestinian, Batwa, African-American, or Muslim. The words of Jesus ring true in my ears: *Anyone* can be my family.

I live with this awareness that the line between family and stranger, mine and not-mine is quite thin. It's so porous, in fact, that we are all just *this close* to belonging to one another. The truth of it—as long as I don't forget it—creates a tenderness in me toward others. It predisposes me to see our commonality, leading me to a greater willingness to walk in solidarity with others both like and unlike me.

They become part of *us*, as Christena Cleveland said. My son, coming home from his first day at a new school with his sister, said it this way: "We agreed to make our own friends, but if anyone tries anything, I got her back and she's got mine." Sibling solidarity is a powerful force on the playground—or at church, or on the streets of Ferguson.

Tenure in the company of the adopted reminds me that we are siblings. This is part of what the Apostle Paul intended us to glean from the adoption metaphor he used in his letters. We are all *adopted ones*, siblings by faith called to love one another, comfort one another, honor and help one another. We are all summoned to a sibling solidarity that is generous, inclusive, and laden with love.

Three months after Claude and I brought our children home, we received visitors. Claude's parents traveled from

Burundi to spend a month in our small home. While they'd given us their blessing as we left Bujumbura, I suspect they came to see how our family was working. I wasn't bothered by their curiosity. I simply welcomed the improved ratio of adults to toddlers—having an African mama on hand could only help our cause, I imagined.

Over the next five weeks I made vats of fresh tomato sauce and white rice, familiar foods for my in-laws. I served up bowls of beans, plates of meat, and frequent apple crisps. My kitchen became the Promised Land, as we went through gallons of milk and several jars of honey to satisfy Mama Rose's craving for tall glasses of honey-sweetened milk.

Amid all the cooking and eating, the kids continued to adjust to their new life. Justin would lean against Claude as he watched the afternoon news. Emma followed Grandpa Andre around, fascinated by him and delighted when he'd drop to the floor to play with her. Mama Rose sat in the rocking chair observing, or sometimes retreated to the patio to get some afternoon sun on her skin. We'd all take turns feeding the kids at dinnertime. No one enjoyed these meals more than my sweet son—more food and more people around the table suited my hungry extrovert. Emma stared at each one of us in turn as she ate.

Later, while Andre and Mama Rose sat in the living room with cups of hot tea, Claude and I would herd the kids into the master bathroom. Each night we'd fill our over-sized tub with warm water, bubble bath, and two toddlers. A cleaning ritual developed as we moved from the tub to towel-drying and christening with lavender lotion. Most nights it was a sacrament, all of us together around the basin, the towel, the blessing of hands anointing one another, the offering of holy butterfly kisses. When our children emerged, clean and shiny, they'd toddle over to their grandparents for more kisses and Kirundi prayers.

Through all those days and nights, Grandpa Andre and Mama Rose witnessed us becoming parents. While they confessed to Claude that they had packed some questions about adopted living when they came to stay with us, they left us knowing that *adopted life* is really another way of saying *family life*.

The night before they left, we took a family photo: my parents, Claude's parents, and our babies all crowded together in the crook of the L-shaped couch. My only regret—no flash. The image was too dark to see what my heart so clearly perceived—we all belonged together.

Not too many weeks later we'd take another family photo, this time in a studio. My mother wanted to start a new family tradition once her grandbabies were home, so she debuted the day-after-Christmas photo shoot. At mother's request, we dressed in shades of chambray and cream for the first sitting. My dad moved around awkwardly, trying to figure out how to hold Emma; my mom tried to coax smiles out of her stiff grandson. Emma proved to be a natural, so photogenic with her long lashes framing her brown eyes and her pinkish lips perfectly curved in a smile. But Justin looked surprised in each picture, like he was caught by the shutter and flash. Claude found it all comical.

Through the years, this tradition has continued. You can tell with each generation of photo that we're more at ease. No one watching the shoot would doubt we're a family, the way we nip at one another, how my dad prods the kids into outbursts of giggles and my mom gets everyone back on track. But when I see the finished product, I'm always amazed at how distinctive our picture is.

From the first candid photo to the last posed picture, I see belonging in every frame. Our family portrait reveals the family God imagined.

There once was a lawyer with a question. (Isn't there always?) This man asked Jesus how he could secure eternal life, what transaction he must perform to ensure his desired outcome. Jesus turned the inquisition back on him: How did *he* read the law? In response the man recited the *shema*: "Love the Lord with all your heart, soul, mind, and strength." Then he added the imperative from Moses to "love your neighbor as yourself." Satisfied with the answer, Jesus seemed to say, in effect, "Yes, go do that!"[1]

But the story isn't over. The lawyer presses for more specifics, testing Jesus. "Who is my neighbor?" It's not an unimportant question.

This ubiquitous imperative to "love your neighbor as yourself" has its roots in Leviticus 19. Moses is addressing the Hebrews at Mount Sinai just on the other side of their exodus from slavery, telling them how to live in relationship with God on this side of freedom. He tells them that holiness includes not hating your kin and loving your neighbor as yourself. In this context the common understanding for neighbor is a fellow Hebrew, someone who shares in the stewardship of the Promised Land.

Then Moses instructs the Hebrews to notice the aliens who reside among them in the land. "Reclassify them as citizens who hold the land in common," he exhorts. Now "they" have become "us." And so Moses circles back and declares that the Hebrews must "love the alien as yourself" to embody holiness in the land that God is giving them. It's a stunning move toward inclusivity for all immigrants. We learn that we must love our kin, obviously, and love our neighbor—and the flip side of that coin is loving the alien who is now a citizen and joint heir. This is how the neighborhood grows wider.

When the lawyer presses Jesus for a better definition of neighbor, Jesus begins telling a story.

There is a man traveling from Jerusalem down to Jericho on a notoriously dangerous road. So it comes as no surprise that he's attacked by violent bandits.[2] They leave him wounded and naked on the roadside. Two holy men, a priest and a Levite, also walking down from their religious duties in Jerusalem, see the man but pass to the other side. Perhaps they're afraid of more bandits lying in wait. But then along comes a third man who, according to the "rule of three" in the way parables work, is the salvific figure of the story. Enter the Samaritan also traveling down to Jericho.

This is the surprise no one saw coming. The bad blood between Jews and Samaritans ran deep and a long way back. Skirmishes across the generations kept Jews and Samaritans apart, despite some shared ancestry,[3] and gave rise to the stereotype of Samaritans as the ever and only dangerous bad guys.

Now all the major players are on the stage. In a recent speech called "Jesus: Best Teacher Ever," New Testament scholar Conrad Gempf made an intriguing observation: with the appearance of a priest and a Levite, we are left to wonder where the Pharisee might be. We might have thought he would be the rescuer, but alas, that hope has been dashed. So, Gempf posited, we must consider the likelihood that he is the one naked and in need of assistance.[4] When you know that a Pharisee and a lawyer are somewhat synonymous, you get the picture. Jesus allows the lawyer in his conversation to become the man in the ditch.

We return to the parable to find that the Samaritan has noticed the beaten man. He goes to him, tends to his wounds, pours oil over him (as both balm and blessing), and puts him on his animal to take him to the nearest inn. At this point the crowd listening in might be catching on.[5] I think Jesus was reminding everyone with ears to hear that there are good Samaritans as well as bad, that not all of them could be tarred with the same brush.

In this parable, as in so many stories, the good guys aren't always good, and the bad guy isn't always bad. Sometimes the people we most fear and vilify can surprise us with compassion.

The more I interact with this parable, the more I begin to see the family resemblance emerge, if imperfectly. These may be siblings in the throes of rivalry, but siblings nonetheless. They are Abraham's children—and occasionally they act like it.

We were hosting a garden party at our home during a Burundian summer—the kind with drummers, dancers, a DJ, and a chef. Most all the guests mingled outside, holding bottles of Fanta and balancing plates loaded with pilau and skewered meats. But inside, seated around the high-top table, Claude and his merry men leaned in and laughed hard. The moment knocked the wind out of me and triggered a memory. I first visited Burundi in September 2001. I was there the day the Twin Towers fell—the day I saw what unbridled hostility looked like. A few years later Claude and I returned to Burundi for the summer. That's when I saw it with different eyes—as an impoverished country with small white mosques popping up in the city and across the countryside. I saw a cocktail for terror.

During a meeting with local pastors, we listened as they shared their grave concern about the increasing Islamic presence in their country. For them, each Muslim embodied a threat to their faith and security. What would happen if their numbers grew? Their tense voices and worry-woven brows made it clear—they were afraid. In retrospect, I realized I was afraid, too.

Since that time, more neighborhood mosques have emerged, dotting the dusty cityscape and punctuating the days with the call to prayer. And since that time, Claude has befriended some Muslim neighbors. Issa owns a local currency exchange bureau in the center of town. He's a good businessman and a faithful family man who offers a gentle grin when you greet him. He's also a devout Muslim. Ndipa operates a car business—buying, selling, and renting. He stands tall above most men. A Muslim father who dotes over his children, he's gregarious and a bit mischievous. On most days Claude visits Issa at work and meets up with Ndipa for a meal. The three of them are always exchanging calls and jokes.

But this posse is incomplete without Rodrigue, Claude's longtime friend, who's always there, the "fixer" of the bunch. He's smooth—the way he laughs, the way his smile steals across his face, the effortless way he gets you out of a jam. Once Catholic, now evangelical . . . he's always been a reliable friend.

And Bahizi joined this group recently. He owns a top-notch construction company and regularly attends a Pentecostal church. He seems attracted to the good humor and good conversation of the other men.

What an odd collective, really. In a country where pastors and imams fear one another, these men are fierce friends. When Rodrigue got married, everyone attended, dressed to the nines. During Ramadan, Issa invites everyone to his home—and we all come. When I arrive at the airport, Ndipa is there to greet me and carry my luggage. These friends have become my family, the people who make me feel welcome and safe in a foreign place.

So when Claude and I throw a garden party, they all come. They bring their wives and children, and they plan to stay awhile. That's why it wasn't unusual to see Claude and his friends together around a table, the Christians with their wine glasses full and the Muslims with their goblets of fruit juice. Except that I recognized something new.

Over the past year, these men had worked alongside Claude to build a school in Bubanza. Issa helped with financing, and Ndipa offered transportation of materials and workers more than once. Bahizi led the construction effort, and Rodrigue worked with the Ministry of Education to secure the license so we could open the school on time. Together this unlikely group brought hope to a desperate place in their country. These Christians and Muslims didn't fight; they collaborated. They weren't afraid of one another; they were friends. These men decided that hospitality trumped hostility.

While local religious leaders gave their energy to anxiety about "the other," these friends gave their energy to neighborliness toward a beleaguered community on the outskirts of town. Together they funded hope instead of fueling fear.

So I watched these men gathered around the table, raising their glasses and doubling over with laughter. And I saw what it looks like to melt swords and fashion them into plowshares. I realized that these men disarmed my own fear, showing me a more excellent way.

Jesus was called a Samaritan once. "Are we not right in saying you are a Samaritan and have a demon?" the Pharisees asked him.

"I do not have a demon," he responded.[6] Still, the religious elite felt justified in their fears of him. They judged him a sinner and a Samaritan, based on the company he kept and where he was from.

During those days, Galilee was a melting pot of sorts, multilingual and full of people who intermarried. If you weren't in a mixed family, you still grew up on streets influenced by them. So Galileans were often called Samaritans—because, who knows, maybe your mother or father came from there. Jesus never refuted the Samaritan slur.

Knowing this makes the parable of the Good Samaritan even more intriguing because perhaps *Jesus* is the Samaritan on the road coming to save those who would prefer to ignore him as insignificant or stone him for blasphemy. I don't actually think that is what Jesus intends as he responds to the questioning lawyer. But all these centuries later, sometimes Jesus and his message of radical inclusion burst into our lives like an unwelcomed kind of salvation from our individualistic and xenophobic ways.

Upon hearing this parable, the lawyer shifts his weight from one leg to the other, trying to relieve his discomfort. The working definition of neighbor that Jesus provides is wider than he imagines or prefers: the neighbor you need might be someone you label as an enemy. Having quoted Leviticus himself, he should have known that immigrants can be citizens and therefore neighbors—which means that now even enemies are neighbors. So all the biblical imperatives about *hesed* and *shalom* apply to, well, everyone.

"Which one of these three was a neighbor to the vulnerable man?" Jesus asks.

"The one who did the act of mercy," the lawyer answers. And so we circle back to the truth that those who keep covenant, those who keep Sabbath, those who live by faith, those who do *hesed* and do the will of the Father—they are covenant neighbors. Isaiah, the magisterial prophet, says that when you clothe the naked, house the homeless, and feed the hungry, you acknowledge them as your kin, your very flesh.

"Go and do likewise," Jesus finally says in answer to the original question. Care for your family here and now—that is how you prepare for the life that is to come. Show compassion here and now to the transcendent family you will share eternity with in the New Jerusalem.

Sometimes a Samaritan can teach us the truth.

Laura and Stuart Wilson's home is my second home, the place where I sink into the couch and easy conversations, laugh louder, and imbibe the goodness of great company. I met Laura—a fellow adoptee, by the way—when I was a college student and she was the administrator for the Communication Studies Department. Once I graduated and stayed on as staff in the Housing Office, Laura and I became colleagues sharing frequent lunches. She was the first Democrat I knew. And contrary to what my conservative parents told me growing up, she was thoughtful and articulate about liberal values.

While Laura was a member at All Saints' by the Sea Episcopal Church, Stuart was a lifelong atheist. This was about all I knew about him before we first met—and it scared me. I remember the first dinner at their home. We sat at their large square table eating grilled chicken and a green salad, passing the bread and butter. Stuart spoke in a gentle rhythm, unhurried and without pretense. I discovered that he was a photographer trained at an elite institute in town, a carpenter by trade, and that his passion was exploring nature—bugs in particular. His favorite hobby combined photography and entomology.

After dinner he brought out a slide projector and screen. We sat in the living room with cups of hot tea as he showed us his recent photographs of katydids, spiders, and wasps. Initially I was amused—close-up glamour shots for bugs! But amusement gave way to fascination as I noticed for the first time the shocking electric green of a katydid, as I saw the fur of the tarantula, the amorous positions of fire ants. Quite simply, Stuart cracked open an entirely new planet for me. At every subsequent dinner I implored him to show me his most recent photos so that I could take in these stunning images and discover more about creatures I often missed—and dismissed—out of disdain, fear, or ignorance.

Stuart took me to my first bug show at the Natural History Museum—an entire auditorium filled with cases of beetles, butterflies, and other insects pinned in place for viewing, with the cases curated by amateur entomologists and enthusiasts. It was the opposite of looking out into the vastness of the Grand Canyon, yet it evoked the same sensation of glorying in God's creation. To be able to appreciate creation's intricacies—this is the lasting gift that Stuart gave to me.

I came of age in evangelical circles where I was taught that Democrats, atheists, and agnostics were to be feared. In the Spirit-filled, non-denominational church we attended, these sorts of people were considered dangerously close to the edge of apostasy (or eternal abyss). I was cautioned to steer clear of them lest I be contaminated by heresies.

Yet without this atheist in my life, I would have missed truly seeing the beauty and truth of creation. Without Stuart, there would be no second home where I'm so easily welcomed. And over the years my husband and children have enjoyed their own moments with Stuart, won over by his kindness and intelligence and enthusiasm for God's creation. He, like Ruth the Moabite, embodies *hesed* to my family. He's shown me the color and texture of creation in golden bees and butterflies, violet lupines and nasturtium.

Though a person claiming no faith, he sees Eden's goodness with more insight and love than most. He's taught me how to better steward God's world and work toward restoration. I cannot imagine the New City without him in it.

Whenever I think about those left out or feared by the dominant culture, I remember Isaiah's words. The Jews have returned home and are working on reconstruction. Based on that current social landscape, certain people had reason to fear exclusion from the new urban enterprise. The foreigners lamented, "Surely the LORD will separate us from his people." According to the law, people with tainted blood and compromised bodies had no place in the Promised Land. And so over time these exclusionary tendencies became the rule—and what Nehemiah reached for when creating the guide for defining covenant neighbors under reconstruction.

Isaiah's poem proposed a radically inclusive policy to counter the fears of the compromised and those considered outcasts. In this poem God tells the eunuchs that they won't be separated out, contrary to Deuteronomy 23; instead, they will carry God's everlasting name into the New City. Then God turns to the immigrants and welcomes them to the holy mountain, saying that they will come with joy into God's house of prayer—which, as we know, will be for all people. This is the declaration of the God Who Gathers, who like a mother hen draws all of them close and calls them "the gathered ones."

God promised Abraham, and Israel, a grand inheritance. Julius Caesar gave his adopted son, Augustus, an imperial inheritance. Jesus was woven into the Davidic dynasty and the heavy lore of that prophetic legacy. Even the Apostle Paul couldn't speak of belonging, of adoption as sons and daughters, without mentioning an accompanying inheritance.

When you belong to a family, you are an heir. You are part of a larger story that reaches back but, more importantly, surges forward. So when Paul says that we are God's adopted ones, and thus full heirs, he is saying that our present reality has huge implications for the future. I'm fond of saying that the New City is that all-inclusive place we're constructing together, but you might call it one body, one family, or God's Kingdom. The point is that we are adopted into this family to enact God's dream for a communion of saints from among the nations. We are heirs apparent to both God's mandate and God's promise. And as heirs, our belonging has no end.

Adoption becomes a perfect metaphor for Paul to continue this conversation about the new family of God. He wanted the church in Rome to see that Jews and Greeks belonged to the same family, that this is the new humanity inaugurated by Christ, shaped by faith and not biology.

The Galatians hear something similar from Paul: that

when the fullness of time came, God sent his Son so we could become God's adopted ones. But not before he reminds them about becoming children of God through faith. Therefore they are no longer categorized as Jew or Greek, male or female, slave or free. All belong to Christ and are Abraham's descendants, and—no surprise—full heirs to the promise. It's the metaphor of adoption which communicates a belonging that supersedes biology, ethnicity, or any kind of binary.

Previously the metaphor of family defined the Jewish self-understanding. There were some variants— thanks to an Egyptian princess, a Moabite mother, and grandsons born on foreign soil—but mostly one's membership was biologically determined. Circumcision offered physical evidence of covenant membership. But Jesus, the Adopted One, subverted the "biology alone" trope. Biology can open but never close the door to membership. Thus, a new family was born for a new kind of humanity.

According to the Apostle Paul's letter to the Ephesian church, God destined us for adoption. God designed a future ripe with belonging where we find one another as siblings and find our way home to our Father's House. It is the mystery revealed "in the fullness of time," the Apostle says, God gathering us all together at long last. We, along with all created on earth and in the heavens, are swept up into God's expansive embrace. It is redemption. It is Jubilee realized. It is the New City descending among us.

For too long we've indulged our exclusivist and exclusionary tendencies, evident in all kinds of faulty determinations. Family is only biological. Connection is only tribal. Ethnicities divide us. Denominational lines of demarcation define us. We wrongly assumed holiness was about individual piety and group purity, missing the communal imperatives to love our neighbor, love the immigrant, even love our enemy. We bristled against such wide inclusion, chafing against acceptance of all others. It was our mistake, a failure of imagination on our part.

Then Jesus came down and walked among us. He showed us how serious he was about kinship. Until then we lacked the sight to see straight. But somehow his adoptive gestures were familiar to us. We began to notice signs of them in Abraham's faith, undeterred by the physicality of circumcision or no circumcision; in Moses' capacity for emancipation as a bicultural leader; in Ruth the Moabite's embodiment of *hesed* and the redemptive reach of Boaz across boundaries to enact Jubilee. And the mothers—how we see belonging gestated by Jochebed and Bithiah and Naomi and Mary! How did we ever miss it—the Spirit weaving this family together? The good news is that we have eyes beginning to see now because the Light of the World has come and shines among us.

Jesus has always been wooing us. We are his adopted ones, the gathered ones, *his kin*. All he has ever wanted was to help us replace our sibling rivalries with brotherly love and sisterly solidarity, to let go of fear in favor of laughter. He invites us to drop our weapons and pick up some silverware because it's time to eat. Ah, the family meal where we are all at home. That is the grace, the sacrament of belonging.

Like any good parent, Jesus wants us to at long last appreciate the goodness of our family. He is the Gathering God, the Adopted One who crosses boundaries to show us that we are all kin despite the ways we differ from each other and even from him. In this fractured world, we belong—that's the truth that binds us to him, Our Father, who art in heaven.

Notes

Notes to Chapter 1

1. Via an email exchange with Brian McLaren in May 2014.

2. Genesis 30:1-3.

3. "... the children of Machir the son of Manasseh were also *born on Joseph's knees*" (Gen. 50:22-23). Andries Van Aarde, author of *Fatherless in Galilee: Jesus as a Child of God* (London: Bloomsbury/T&T Clark), writes, "The reference would in this case be to a father who took the child onto his knees as an indication that he recognized the child as his own" (p. 175).

4. Ruth 4:13-17. The text goes on to say that the women of the village said, "A son has been born to Naomi." This sounds like an adoption formula—the recognition that the child is now hers and thus a full heir.

5. In Hebrews 5:8 we are told that Jesus "learned obedience." I imagine it was one of many things he learned during his earthly tenure.

6. Van Aarde, *Fatherless in Galilee*, p. 176.

7. To learn more about the social dynamics of group formation as they affect the church, read Christena Cleveland's *Disunity in Christ: Uncovering the Hidden Forces That Keep Us Apart* (Downers Grove, IL: InterVarsity Press, 2013).

Notes to Chapter 2

1. Antjie Krog, *Country of My Skull: Guilt, Sorrow, and the Limits of Forgiveness in the New South Africa* (New York: Broadway Books, 2000).

Notes to Chapter 4

1. Leonardo Boff, *Holy Trinity, Perfect Community* (Maryknoll, NY: Orbis Books, 2000), p. 38.

2. Genesis 18:1-8.

3. Richard Rohr's comments on the Trinity and the Rublev icon can also be found in his book *The Divine Dance: The Trinity and Your Transformation* (New Kensington, PA: Whitaker House, 2016).

4. This is Richard Rohr's description of the activity of the Trinity during "Richard Rohr and the Alternative Orthodoxy" on The RobCast aired on April 10, 2016.

5. Luke 14:1-14.

6. Desmond Tutu, *God Is Not a Christian: And Other Provocations* (New York: Harper One, 2011), p. 21, and *No Future without Forgiveness* (New York: Image Books, 2000), p. 31.

7. Tutu, *No Future without Forgiveness*, p. 265.

8. Boff, *Holy Trinity, Perfect Community*, p. 71.

9. Tutu, *God Is Not a Christian*, p. 22.

10. Tim Keel of Jacob's Well in Kansas City and author of *Intuitive Leadership: Embracing a Paradigm of Narrative, Metaphor, and Chaos* (Grand Rapids: Baker Books, 2007).

11. Tutu, *No Future without Forgiveness*, p. 265.

Notes to Chapter 5

1. Latin American theologians use the word *accompaniment* to talk about a deep solidarity and partnership with the poor. The works of Gustavo Gutiérrez and Jon Sobrino are good introductions to this way of re-

flecting on our work alongside the poor. The Tarmans and Hernandezes embody this practice with fidelity and grace.

2. I'm grateful to my friend Kent Annan for this rich phrase describing the tension between the now and the not yet of God's Kingdom. His book by the same name shares his own journey of brokenness, redemption, and the work of justice in Haiti. See *Slow Kingdom Coming* (Downers Grove, IL: InterVarsity Press, 2016).

3. Ruth 1:16–17.

4. I'm indebted to the scholarship and interpretive work of Ellen Davis with regard to my own thoughts on the story of Ruth. Her book, *Who Are You, My Daughter? Reading Ruth through Image and Text* (Philadelphia: Westminster John Knox Press, 2016), is a treasure trove.

5. Romans 8:23.

6. It is for this reason that John Dominic Crossan calls the book of Ruth a challenge parable. This story challenges the demand for ethnic purity, and thus hatred of the Moabites most of all, depicted in Nehemiah and Ezra. See *The Power of Parable: How Fiction* by *Jesus Became Fiction* about *Jesus* (New York: HarperOne, 2013), pp. 69–75.

7. Ruth 4:5.

8. Ruth 2:20.

Notes to Chapter 6

1. *Tikkun olam* is found in the Kabbalah. It has a wide semantic range, from the straightforward sense of social justice to the more mystical notion of imagining pieces of glory scattered across the world which must be reclaimed to fully restore glory's divine intent. The term is both revered and contested. Some think it has been overused and misused and is itself beyond repair. Others find it worth reclaiming.

2. Ezekiel 34:25–29a as translated by Walter Brueggemann in *Living toward a Vision: Biblical Reflections on Shalom*, 2nd ed. (Cleveland: Pilgrim Press, 1982), p. 16.

3. Walter Brueggemann, *Peace* (Atlanta: Chalice Press, 2001), p. 15. The entire book is an accessible and fairly comprehensive exploration of biblical *shalom*.

4. In Isaiah 58 we see clearly that the quality of life in Jerusalem is unraveling because, as the prophet notes, the employers don't pay a fair wage to their employees. Once the economic practices are adjusted toward justice for all workers and communities begin working together on local infrastructure projects, God will speak to them again.

5. See Leviticus 25, Deuteronomy 15, Isaiah 61, and Luke 4.

6. Leviticus 25:10 reads: "And you shall hallow the fiftieth year and you shall proclaim liberty throughout the land to all its inhabitants. It shall be a jubilee for you: you shall return, every one of you, to your property and *every one of you to your family*" (italics mine).

7. Samuel L. Adams, in *Social and Economic Life in Second Temple Judea,* posits that the prohibition against intermarriage may have been due to economic factors as much as concerns about social separation. Mixed marriages might have allowed land to fall into foreign hands, so the prohibition could have been about protecting holy seed and holy lands. Again, economics impinge on family formation.

Notes to Chapter 7

1. The Synoptic writers all note this declaration of sonship by the heavenly Voice. John's Gospel veers, saying that Jesus' divine status as the Son of God was revealed to the crowd.

2. Andries van Aarde speaks of how fatherhood is articulated throughout Judaism and within the Gospels. See his book *Fatherless in Galilee: Jesus as Child of God* (London: T & T Clark, 2001), pp. 138ff., 150.

3. This poem was tweeted out on the evening of May 30, 2016, and then published on Lisa Sharon Harper's Facebook account on May 31, 2016.

4. Read Naim Stifan Ateek's chilling account of his own family history in his masterful work *Justice and Only Justice: A Palestinian Theology of Liberation* (Maryknoll, NY: Orbis Books, 1989).

5. See Proverbs 13:12: "Hope deferred makes the heart sick, but a desire fulfilled is a tree of life."

6. Revelation 21 speaks of this new city descending: 21:1-2 about the

old passing away and the new descending, and 21:25 confirming the ever-open gates.

7. Isaiah 56:7.

Notes to Chapter 8

1. This story is told in Luke 10:25–37.

2. In his book *Bandits, Prophets, and Messiahs: Popular Movements at the Time of Jesus*, Richard A. Horsley explores the banditry of this parable. It is highly likely this was a Robin Hood scenario, where the economically disadvantaged bandits overtook the well-off traveler. Taking his money, even his clothes, would have been seen as justice, since his wealth was ill-gotten. Often these bandits distributed the money to their village. This social reality points to the possibility that the traveler in the parable was, like the lawyer posing the initial question, rich by means that exploited the peasants. The possibilities of the plot thicken. . . .

3. The Samaritans are believed to have descended from the Patriarch Joseph's sons, Ephraim and Manasseh.

4. You can find the speech at http://simplyjesusgathering.com/jesus -best-teacher-ever-conrad-gempf/.

5. The lawyer schooled in the old stories sees the connection. All the plot points match the narrative found in 2 Chronicles 28:8-15: Jericho, Samaria, blessings, beasts of burden, and the people from the north and the south kingdoms (now known as Samaritans and Jews). The two kingdoms were at war, and the Jewish people of the south got trounced by their northern neighbors, aka the Samaritans. The Jews were rounded up and marched from Jericho toward Samaria as booty, slated for slavery. But Oded the prophet spoke a word of the Lord to the Samaritan leaders, telling them to let the Jews from the south go. After the generals agreed, the Samaritan soldiers tended to the needs of their Jewish captives, clothed them, blessed them, put the feeble ones on animals, and allowed them all to return to Jericho. In this instance further violence and enslavement were thwarted, and good Samaritans revealed.

6. John 8:48.

Acknowledgments

The first thing I learned as I began the adventure of writing this book was the importance of the partnership between writer and editor. D. L. Mayfield and Amy Peterson, my first editors, taught me how to receive critique as a constructive gift. Without compensation beyond my gratitude, they edited each chapter. With each set of honest notes, they made me feel deeply seen and deeply loved. Lil Copan pushed me to be bold with her generous, fearless, and fierce brilliance. Her skills made her the perfect midwife for this book; she offered support and confidence in turn. Mary Hietbrink tightened syntax and foraged for the precise word to ensure clarity paragraph by paragraph. These women taught me that writing is a collaborative endeavor, pen and pruning hook working together to bring a bounty of goodness to the reader's table. For these partners, I give thanks.

Beyond my circle of editors stood my sisters of holy mischief, my faithful band of writing friends: Jessica Goudeau,

Stina Kielsmeier-Cook, D. L. Mayfield, Amy Peterson, and Christiana Peterson. Through the ebb and flow of the writing months, the editing months, and the fallow times in between, these women patiently listened, gently chided, offered comfort, and cheered in celebration. They remind me of the old African proverb: *If you want to go fast, go alone. If you want to go far, go together.* They walked the distance with me, and for that I give them a hearty word of thanksgiving.

The first time I ventured to write a public word about adoption back in the summer of 2012, these three friends were with me: Sarah Bessey, Idelette McVicker, and Sherry Naron. They haven't left my side since. No one has weathered more of my highest hopes and darkest fears about this project than these friends. They've been my bulwark against storms of insecurity and writing impasses. They've given me a safe place to rest and reminded me to trust each step of the way. In these women, God has given me three sisters, and I am ever grateful.

Alongside editors, a writing group, and sisters have stood two other women I remain in debt to for all the best reasons. Rachelle Gardner has been more than a literary agent. Yes, she educated me at each turn, advocated for me, and found me the best publishing house. But best of all, she's become a friend I enjoy laughing with over a good meal as we share our stories and our hopes. Diana Trautwein has been my spiritual companion ever since I began this project.

Inviting her to care for my soul amid the publishing process was a stroke of spirit-breathed genius. How good it is to have someone loving and praying you through, ensuring that publication could simultaneously be spiritual formation. What a blessing to have these women alongside me.

I must share my appreciation for the many other friends who offered moral and tangible support during the writing of this book: Laura Shook, Brian McLaren, Laura Wilson, Nish Weiseth, Seth and Amber Haines, Jason and Heather Sunukjian, Sean and Paige Whiting, and Shane and Anastasia Wilson. And I cannot leave out the hometown team that kept me caffeinated and full of good cheer as I worked—the quick-witted baristas and beloved regulars at my local Starbucks in Surprise, Arizona. There were also portions written in Le Beryl Café and edited in Café Gourmand in my other hometown of Bujumbura, Burundi. I guess I've also learned that alongside good people, a good place to work makes a big difference!

The culmination of my gratitude belongs to Claude Nikondeha: a man of peace, a friend to the poor, and an entrepreneur of hope. I could ask for no better partner in this life or in this work than him. He's the one creating space for me to write, going to great lengths and allowing me to live at great distances from him to grow this work in the most fertile land. He pushes me forward and inspires me. I also appreciate the sacrifice my children, Justin and

Acknowledgments

Emma, have made as I worked away from home or clois-
tered in my room to coax words and make deadlines. They
became co-encouragers, and I hope they are proud of our
story. And thanks to Art and Madelyn Johnson, who welcomed me home one April day in 1969. You taught me what
belonging looks like and set my trajectory for a new story.

KELLEY NIKONDEHA
Adoption Day
April 2017